T0163048

An Italian Pantry

Carla Bardi

Prosciutto

An Italian Pantry

WINE APPRECIATION GUILD

Also available in
"An Italian Pantry":

OLIVE OIL

CHEESE

PASTA

First Published in North America 2004
The Wine Appreciation Guild
360 Swift Avenue
South San Francisco CA 94080

ISBN 1-891267-54-X

This book was conceived, edited and designed by
McRae Books Srl, Florence, Italy.

Publishers: Anne McRae, Marco Nardi
Text: Carla Bardi
Photography: Marco Lanza, Walter Mericchi
Set Design: Rosalba Gioffrè
Design: Marco Nardi
Layout: Adriano Nardi
Translation from the Italian: Marilena Cairns
Editing: Anne McRae

2 4 6 8 10 9 7 5 3 1

Color separations: Fotolito Toscana, Florence, Italy
Printed and bound in China

Contents

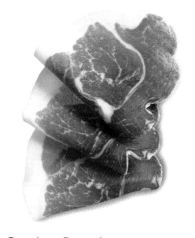

Introduction

The original Italian title of this book is *Salumi*, a generic term that covers a vast array of different meats that have been cured with salt and spices then cooked or dried. Alongside a few already well known meats such as *prosciutto crudo di Parma* (Parma ham), cooked ham, pancetta, and mortadella (sometimes called Bologna sausage in English), we have sought out a host of regional specialties, many of which have only recently become known outside their zones of origin.

The majority of Italian deli meats are made using pork. Every edible part of the animal, including trotters, jowls, fat, and the skin, is processed in one way or another to obtain smoked, steamed, cooked, or dried deli meats. To a much lesser extent, other meats are also used, including beef, goose, turkey, horse, wild boar, and venison.

Producing tasty deli meats is an art. Relying on knowledge acquired over the centuries, skilled producers use just the right amounts of salt, spices, and other aromas to process and preserve the meat. Many Italian deli meats are made in very specific areas of the country, where the local climate is the only one that can produce the inimitable scent and flavor of the finished products.

Italian deli meats are divided into two main groups, known as *insaccati* and *salumi*. The first group includes all salamis, sausages, and everything else which is packed into natural or synthetic animal gut. The second group includes meats that are preserved without being wrapped in gut, such as pancetta or lard.

Above: The term deli meats refers to a wide range of salamis, air-dried and cooked hams, sausages, and other, predominantly pork, products. All deli meats can be served with a glass of good Italian wine.

Below: a selection of regional products from Emilia-Romagna. Many of the best known deli meats come from Emila-Romagna in northern Italy. This region, as well as being the home of world renown Parmesan cheese, balsamic vinegar, and many fresh and stuffed pasta shapes, including tortellini, has also given us mortadella, Parma ham, zampone, and cotechino.

D.O.P.(denominazione di origine protetta) and I.G.P. (indicazione geografica protetta)

The government of the European Community has issued quite strict regulations designed to protect regional food products. It has established two labels, D.O.P. and I.G.P. which are recognized throughout the Community. Through GATT agreements this recognition has been extended throughout the world.

The D.O.P. label *(denominazione di origine protetta)*, that can be translated literally as "denomination of protected origin," designates a product as coming from a specific area in which the local environment (including both natural and human factors) leads to a unique product. The entire production process must take place within the designated area.
The I.G.P. *(indicazione geografica protetta)* label is a new guarantee of quality that focuses more on the production processes than the geographical area itself. It is used to identify a product from a specific region, the quality, reputation, and characteristics of which can only be traced to that area. At least one phase in the production process must also take place within the designated area.

Both labels are intended to provide consumers with a guarantee of quality since they know that the item they are buying has been produced in a restricted area according to precise regulations. The labels also help protect products and the people who produce them, ensuring that they don't die out and are not imitated by inferior or mass produced items.

ITALIAN D.O.P. DELI MEATS

Type	Production Zone
Prosciutto di Parma	Emila-Romagna
Prosciutto di San Daniele	Friuli
Prosciutto di Modena	Emila-Romagna
Prosciutto Berico-Euganeo	Veneto
Prosciutto di Carpegna	The Marches
Prosciutto Toscano	Tuscany
Salame di Varzi	Emilia-Romagna
Salame di Brianza	Lombardy
Salame Piacentino	Emilia-Romagna
Culatello di Zibello	Emilia-Romagna
Jambon de Bosses	Val d'Aosta
Lard d'Arnad	Val d'Aosta
Coppa Piacentina	Emilia-Romagna
Pancetta Piacentina	Emilia-Romagna
Soppressata di Calabria	Calabria
Capocollo di Calabria	Calabria
Salsiccia di Calabria	Calabria
Pancetta di Calabria	Calabria

ITALIAN I.G.P. DELI MEATS

Type	Production Zone
Speck dell'Alto Adige	Alto Adige
Bresaola della Valtellina	Lombardy
Prosciutto di Norcia	Umbria
Mortadella Bologna	Emilia-Romagna
Zampone Modena	Emilia-Romagna
Cotechino Modena	Emilia-Romagna

The Story of Prosciutto

The use of salt to preserve meat is an ancient tradition. The Roman statesman and prose writer Cato (above), writing in about 160 BC in his De agri cultura, outlines salting and drying procedures that are very similar to those still in use today.

Below: Delicious Parma ham served with piadina, an unleavened bread from the coastal region of Emila-Romagna, and a local fresh cheese. Since the ancient Romans ate unleavened bread, this modern dish may be very similar to what Hannibal was served more than 2,200 years ago!

The origins of prosciutto making in Italy date back at least to Roman and Etruscan times, if not before. In the 2nd century BC, Cato the Elder, author of *De agri cultura*, the oldest surviving complete work in Latin, described how a delicious ham of pork was preserved by being first salted, then dried and rubbed with olive oil. Since the process is not unlike the one used today to make *prosciutto crudo* (raw ham, such as Parma ham), this is generally believed to be an early form of prosciutto. Salami is also deeply rooted in Italian gastronomic history and was made both by the Etruscans and the Romans. However, it seems that salami was not invented in Italy since wall paintings showing salami-like meats in the tomb of the Egyptian pharaoh Ramses III (1182–1151 BC) suggest that it was already known in the Egyptian world.

Another Roman scholar and satirist, Marcus Terentius Varro (116–27 BC), in his treatise *De re rustica* ("Farm Topics") says that the Gauls (French Celts) were the most expert when it came to preserving pork meat and that the Romans imported it in large quantities from the Gauls who lived in what is now northern Italy. The Greek historians Polybius and Strabo, who both wrote extensively on early Roman civilization, confirm this opinion. According to legend, during the Second Punic War after the historic battle on the banks of the Trebia River in 217 BC, the victorious Hannibal entered the city of Parma where he was warmly greeted by the locals. Despite the fact that it was the dead of winter and the Romans had requisitioned almost everything in their efforts to fight off the Carthaginians, a great banquet was prepared in his honor. The local peasants brought out hams preserved in salt which they had hidden away from the Romans. Hannibal is said to have greatly appreciated this tasty meat.

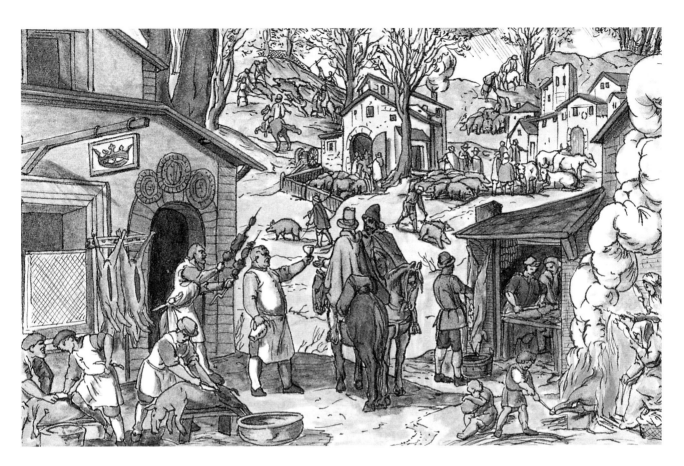

The origins of mortadella can also be traced to Roman times or even earlier. The Romans were extremely fond of *"farcimen myrtatum,"* which was made with pork meat ground in a mortar, then cooked and flavored with myrtle. Although this is clearly an ancestor of modern mortadella, it was not until 1661 that Cardinal Farnese in Bologna published a ban that codified the production of this deli meat.

Pork is the main ingredient in almost all deli meats. Hypocrates, often known as "the father of medicine," wrote in the 5th century BC that "pork is the meat that gives the most strength to the human body and is easy to digest." A few centuries later, Pliny the Elder wrote in his *Natural History,* "No animal provides more material to please the palate: pork meat offers at least fifty different tastes, while every other animal has just one flavor."

Above: This 16th-century illustration shows the various stages of butchering pigs.

Below: A selection of fresh Tuscan deli meats.

Above: Selection of cured meats and sausages in a butcher's shop in Greve. The salamini piccanti (spicy little salamis) in the foreground are made by adding hot chili peppers to the meat mixture before curing.

During the Middle Ages, the Lombards, a Germanic people who migrated into northern Italy from Germany during the 6th century, were known to consume large quantities of pork made from wild boar. What they could not eat fresh was treated with salt and transformed into lard, prosciutto, ham, and various types of sausages and salami. During the early Middle Ages salt was particularly expensive since it had to be transported from the coast. The Lombards were lucky because they were able to use salt from local sources, especially from Salsomaggiore, near Parma.

Records of various kinds show that deli meats continued to be produced all over Italy throughout the the Middle Ages and the Renaissance. Production was mainly at a local level with the meats being eaten in the villages and towns where they were made. A few deli meats did go further afield, some in quite interesting ways! Documents dating to the turn of the 18th century show that pirates from Genoa set out on their six-month long raids loaded up with Parma ham and other deli meat delicacies from Emilia-Romagna and the Veneto. Apart from revealing the pirates' refined culinary tastes, these long-life meats were obviously ideal for lengthy sea voyages, particularly among those whose livelihoods made them unwelcome in most ports!

Above: One of the most highly prized and expensive of all Italian deli meats is made in the area around the little town of Zibello, in the province of Parma. Known as culatello, it is made from the upper part of the pig's leg, which is boned, seasoned with salt, garlic, pepper, and other spices, and then folded and sewn into its own skin. Thinly sliced, it is served as an appetizer.

Gradually, some Italian deli meats became known abroad. By the beginning of the 19th century, Parma ham was much sought after by connoisseurs of fine foods in Paris. It's fame was spread by two Italian musicians of the period – Rossini and Paganini. Rossini was renown for his refined palate and also as a great chef (many of his recipes made use of prosciutto from his native Emilia), while Paganini attributed his rapid recovery from ill-health to the benefits brought about by consuming Italian prosciutto.

Below: A proud Tuscan butcher shows off his freshly made sausages in his store in Greve, in Chianti.

But there are anecdotes to be told about almost all the different meats. Speck, which originated in the alpine villages of Alto Adige, is said to have been invented to conserve meat through the long winter months, when it was the peasants' only source of protein.

In recent years, as strict health regulations have been introduced by European Union lawmakers, many small producers have been threatened because their centuries-old production methods do not conform to 21st-century standards. Fortunately, pressure groups have sprung up to make their products known and to protect them from unnecessarily severe regulations.

The Production Process

Above: Wild boars roam freely in many parts of Italy and they are used in a range of regional specialties, including deli meats. This large male boar was photographed in Maremma, the wild coastal strip in southern Tuscany.

Below: These antique illustrations show how pigs were butchered in the past. Then, as now, no part of the animal was wasted.

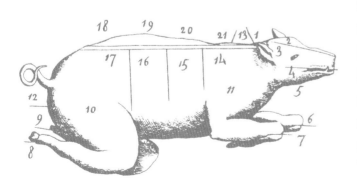

P ig farming in Italy differs notably from other European countries, especially in the central and northern parts of the peninsula. In the rest of Europe, pigs are usually butchered at less than 220 lb (100 kg), whereas most pigs in Italy are destined for the deli meats industry which requires more mature meat with a higher fat content that will not dry out too much during processing. Italian pigs are bred, raised, fed, and butchered with this in mind. The ideal animal has been well defined: it should be large, with a uniform pale pink skin and white bristles. It should have a compact body structure, be well muscled, and have a robust skeleton and legs. Its backbone should arch slightly and it should possess a vigorously curled tail attached well up on the hindquarters.

Once the ideal pig has been raised, the next important steps involve how it is slaughtered and how the cuts are processed and preserved. Each phase is crucial; the animal must be kept alive until the right moment, and the carcass has to be protected from loss of weight in the form of liquids, fat, or muscle. Bad or unskilled butchering can lead to inferior meats with a range of more or less serious defects.

The best pork for making deli meats is compact and an even light-red in color. The different types of deli meats are made from various parts of the carcass (what is left of the animal once the blood and internal organs have been removed). The carcass is divided into pieces cut according to how they are destined to be processed. The way the carcass is divided varies greatly from one region to another. The head is used to make *guanciale*, which is cut in a triangular shape from the throat, cheeks, and part of the neck. The other parts, and the cheeks themselves when guanciale is not being made, are used to produce zampone, cotechino, and soppressato. The shoulders are used to make coppa, capocollo, or ham, or can be ground to make salami. The skin can also be used to wrap zampone. Choice cuts from the body are ground and used to make high quality salami and sausages. The hindquarters, or hams, are used to make prosciutto crudo, or can be turned into ham, culatello, fiocco, and speck. Fat from different parts of the body is used to make guanciale, lard, and pancetta. Lard is usually made from fat cut from the animal's back, while pancetta is cut from the belly. The trimmings are used to fill salami. Lard can be chopped into cubes or small pieces and used to make sausages, salami, and mortadella.

Generally speaking, Italian deli meats produced in the warmer, southern regions are more flavorsome, while these from cooler regions are more delicate in taste. Many factors play a role in the processing of a high quality deli meat, from a correct working method, to cooking, smoking, or steaming (where applicable), curing with salt, choice of spices, skilled handling of aging or drying, and careful warehousing, packaging, and transportation to retail outlets. Nature's contribution to many of these steps is of fundamental importance. Some local microclimates are crucial in conferring a special perfume or taste to many Italian deli meats. They provide that added extra that can change a deli meat from being ordinary into something very unique and special that can only be obtained in certain geographical areas.

Above: An early 20th-century advertisement for a deli meat maker in Piedmont.

Below: Quality control in a Parma ham factory in Emilia-Romagna. Ongoing improvement in the techniques used to make Italian deli meats has led to products of much higher quality.

Serving Prosciutto

Until recently, asking for an *antipasto* (appetizer) in Italy would almost certainly mean that you would be brought a selection of sliced deli meats with a basket of fresh bread. In season, you could expect the *prosciutto crudo* to be accompanied by some juicy wedges of cantaloupe (melon), while salami might be served with fresh figs. The meats might also be accompanied by a selection of *crostini* with liver pâté, chopped tomato and garlic, and boiled cannellini or other beans. Nowadays the range of antipasti is much larger and often more sophisticated, although deli meats remain a staple.

During the summer and fall, do try serving prosciutto crudo and salami with fresh fruit. Cantaloupe and figs are obvious choices, but you can also be more adventurous. Kiwi fruit are particularly good, but a range of other fresh and dried fruits can also be tried. In Tuscany and other parts of central Italy, local deli meats are often served with slices of Pecorino cheese. This is a rather filling appetizer, so you may prefer to serve it as a light lunch or snack. In that case, prepare a green salad or some lightly steamed vegetables to accompany the deli meats. Freshly baked bread is a must with this combination.

With the exception of some large sausages from Emilia-Romagna (zampone and cotechino), most deli meats are served without being cooked. However, we have included many recipes, both traditional and modern, which make use of deli meats in cooked dishes.

As a general rule, rosé wines go well with most deli meats. We have included a wine recommendation with each dish.

Prosciutto Crudo Dolce

The salted, air-dried hams used to make *prosciutto crudo dolce* (literally, "sweet raw ham"), are obtained from the hindquarters of pigs weighing about 350 lb (170 kg). The meat is a bright, rosy color, lightly veined with fat. The hams are treated with an energetic salt massage before undergoing about 12 months of drying in well-ventilated storerooms. Every region of Italy produces its own special prosciutto crudo. The best-known of the "sweet" types are San Daniele, made in Friuli in the north, and Parma, made in Emilia-Romagna in northern Italy.

MAIN PRODUCTION ZONES: Friuli-Venezia Giulia (San Daniele) and Emilia-Romagna (Parma)

MADE FROM: pork (hindquarters of well-grown pigs)

CURING AGENTS: salt

AGING: San Daniele at least 12 months

Parma 10–12 months

Flavor: almost sweet, buttery

The trotter left on the ham is a distinctive feature of San Daniele ham.

San Daniele hams are fire branded with a legally-recognized trademark that represents the stylized image of a ham with the letters SD surrounded by the name PROSCIUTTO DI SAN DANIELE

San Daniele

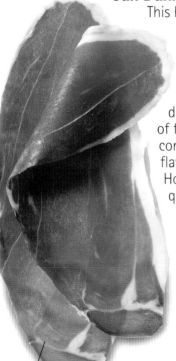

This ham is made in the San Daniele and Sauris regions of Friuli. It is cured on the bone and the hams are pressed, making them longer and leaner than the Parma variety. The pressing process is done to obtain a better distribution of fat and lean meat. Many connoisseurs prefer the distinctive flavor of San Daniele to Parma ham. However, it is produced in smaller quantities and can be expensive.

Sweet raw ham has a fragrant odor and a delicate, not-too-salty, flavor. Tasty and aromatic, it is especially good when served with fruit (cantaloupe, figs) or lightly steamed or boiled delicately-flavored vegetables, such as asparagus.

The thinly sliced ham must be rosy red, with very little fat in the meat and just a thin layer of fat running around the outside.

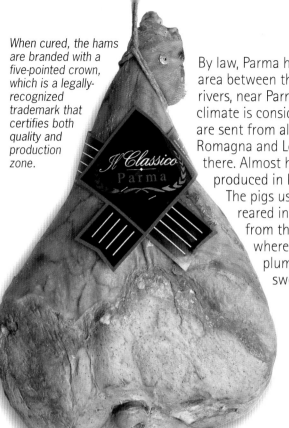

When cured, the hams are branded with a five-pointed crown, which is a legally-recognized trademark that certifies both quality and production zone.

Parma

By law, Parma ham must be cured in the area between the Taro and Baganza rivers, near Parma. The local climate is considered ideal and hams are sent from all over Emilia-Romagna and Lombardy to be cured there. Almost half of all the raw ham produced in Italy comes from this area. The pigs used to make the ham are reared indoors, and are fed on whey from the local cheese factories (this is where Parmesan cheese is made). The plump Parma hams have a very mild and sweet flavor.

Parma ham should be served very thinly sliced. Try to buy slices from the center of the ham; the end parts are tougher and saltier.

Risotto with Mascarpone and Prosciutto
(Serves 4–6)

Ingredients
- 1 medium white onion, cut in 4 wedges
- 3 oz/90 g butter
- 13 oz/400 g short-grain rice (preferably Italian Arborio or Carnaroli)
- 1 cup/ 250 ml dry white wine
- 4 cups/1 liter meat stock (homemade or stock cube)
- 4 oz/125 g prosciutto crudo dolce
- salt and freshly ground black pepper to taste
- 5 oz/150 g Mascarpone cheese
- 4 tbsp extra-virgin olive oil

In a heavy-bottomed pan, sauté the onion in half the butter until soft. Discard the onion and add the remaining butter. Melt over high heat. When it is bubbling, add the rice, pour in the wine, and stir until it evaporates. Add enough stock to cover the rice, and bring to a boil. Stir, almost constantly, adding more stock as the rice absorbs it, until tender. When the rice is almost cooked, add the prosciutto, season with salt and pepper, stir in the Mascarpone, and drizzle with the oil. The risotto should be moist and creamy. Serve hot.

Wine: a light, dry red (Rosso Piceno)

Prosciutto Crudo Salato

PROSCIUTTO CRUDO SALATO

MAIN PRODUCTION ZONES: Tuscany, Umbria (Norcia), Marches (Montefeltro)
MADE FROM: pork (hindquarters of pigs)
CURING AGENTS: salt, pepper, herbs, and spices
AGING: 12–18 months
FLAVOR: full, persistent

Typical of central and southern Italy, this salty, raw ham has a strong, savory taste. It differs from the hams produced in northern Italy because the warmer southern climate requires more salt in the curing process. These hams are cured using a mixture of salt and pepper (often flavored with herbs and spices), which imparts a very full and persistent flavor, particularly in hams that have been aged for longer than 18 months. Tuscan raw ham has an especially strong flavor that goes very well with the local unsalted bread. Norcia ham, made in Umbria, is another well-known variety. It is cured with salt, pepper, and garlic. Ham from Montefeltro, in the Marches, is washed with hot water to remove the salt and then left to dry for about 3 months in a warm and slightly smokey storeroom. Once dry, it is washed with cooked wine and treated with a mixture of laurel, garlic, sugar, and rosemary. It is then covered with ground pepper.

18

Tuscan ham carries a D.O.P. label (see introduction).

There are many quite fanciful theories for why Tuscan bread is traditionally made without salt. However, the most logical explanation is that local products, such as raw ham, have very strong, salty flavors which are best eaten with plain-tasting bread.

Tuscan ham is best served when carved from the ham by hand in fairly thick slices.

Prosciutto with Cantaloupe (Serves 4)

Ingredients
- 12 slices raw ham (sweet or salty)
- 1 medium cantaloupe (melon)

Rinse the cantaloupe and cut it in half. Slice each half into 4 to 6 wedges and arrange them on a serving dish with the ham.

Wine: a dry, aromatic white (Malvasia del Collio)

Cinta Senese ham can be distinguished by its smaller than normal size, and by the bristles left on the skin. The animal's dark trotter is left attached to the ham.

Prosciutto di Cinta Senese

The Cinta Senese is an ancient breed of pig from the province of Siena, in Tuscany. Very dark in color, it is named for the white strip on its shoulders and forelegs (called a "cinta" or belt). It was raised in the province of Siena and the whole Chianti area from the Middle Ages until the 1950s when it was replaced by larger, modern breeds. Rediscovered recently, its ham has a very intense, savory flavor that goes perfectly with the local breads and the "rough" Chianti wines.

The Cinta pigs are raised almost in the wild, which makes the meat particularly tasty. When sliced, it is a bright orange-brown color, with most of the fat lying on the outside near the skin. With a strong aroma, it is savory without being too salty.

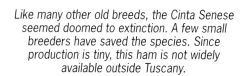

Like many other old breeds, the Cinta Senese seemed doomed to extinction. A few small breeders have saved the species. Since production is tiny, this ham is not widely available outside Tuscany.

Prosciutto di Norcia

Norcia ham is known as "mountain ham" because once it has been treated with salt (and pepper in the areas not covered by skin), it is cured slowly in the thin, dry air of the Umbrian hills. There are two types: the *"tipico di Norcia,"* which is dried for 12 months, and the *"antico di Norcia,"* made by local artisans according to ancient traditions, which is dried for 24 months. Norcia hams have a distinctive pear shape. Great care is taken in its curing and drying. Once the hams have been pressed and the skins removed from the inner parts, they are cured with salt, pepper, and garlic and then left to rest for 20 to 30 days, depending on their weight. They are then washed with warm water and wine and then treated again with pepper and garlic. They are then hung to dry and just lightly smoked. After about 8 months, they are covered in a mixture of lard and flour and left to dry in the cool, fairly humid mountain air until ready.

Norcia ham is a fairly dark, almost ruby red. It poses some resistance to the bite, but the time taken to chew it gives you the chance to appreciate its full, pungent flavors.

Medallions of Ham with Broccoli and Anchovies
(Serves 6)

Ingredients
- 12 slices prosciutto salata, about 2¹/₂ oz/75 g each
- 5 oz/150 g Mozzarella cheese, thinly sliced
- 1 tbsp capers
- 12 spicy green olives, pitted, and cut in half
- salt and freshly ground black pepper
- 6 slices pancetta, unrolled
- 2 cloves garlic, finely chopped
- 3 sage leaves, finely chopped
- 1 sprig rosemary, finely chopped
- ¹/₂ cup/125 ml dry white wine
- 1¹/₂ lb/750 g broccoli, lightly boiled, in florets
- 6 tbsp extra-virgin olive oil
- 6 anchovy fillets

Lightly pound the prosciutto with a meat pounder. Arrange the Mozzarella, capers, and olives on 6 of the 12 pieces. Lightly season with salt and cover with the remaining slices of pork. Roll each one up in a slice of pancetta and secure with a wooden toothpick. Place in a skillet (frying pan) with a little water over low heat. Add the garlic, sage, rosemary, and a dash of pepper. When the pancetta is lightly browned, drizzle with the wine and cook until it evaporates. In a separate pan, dissolve the anchovies in the oil and sauté the broccoli for 5 minutes. Serve the medallions hot with the broccoli.

Wine: a dry red (Carmignano Rosso)

20

Culatello

Considered the king of Italian deli meats, culatello is obtained from the muscle on the upper part of a pig's ham. The skin and bone are removed and the remaining meat is used to make less prestigious products, called *fiocchetto* and *cappello del prete*. Culatello is produced only in the tiny Bassa Verdiana area (also the birthplace of Giuseppe Verdi) in the province Parma, where the local climate (cold and damp in the winter, hot and humid in the summer) ensures perfect curing conditions.

MAIN PRODUCTION ZONES: Emilia-Romagna (Parma)
MADE FROM: pork (muscular parts of hindquarters)
CURING AGENTS: salt, pepper, spices, and wine
AGING: 10–12 months
FLAVOR: delicate, subtle

Parma
EMILIA-ROMAGNA

Curing

The meat for culatello is treated with salt and spices soon after the pig is butchered. It is then wrapped in the animal's bladder and tied with string. Compared to Parma ham, which requires cool, dry air to cure, culatello needs humidity to soften the fat-free meat and to develop its full blend of subtle flavors. The average culatello weighs 11 lb (5 kg) before curing, which is reduced by almost half when the meat is ready after about a year.

Sometimes culatello is wrapped in a cloth dampened with white wine to conserve humidity.

21

Culatello has a complex and refined bouquet, and is best savored in this simple dish.

Culatello with Butter
(Serves 4)

Ingredients
• 12 thin slices culatello
• 3 oz/90 g butter, chopped

Place the culatello on a serving dish and sprinkle with the butter. Serve with fresh, crusty bread.
Wine: a dry red (Gutturno)

Prosciutto Cotto

PROSCIUTTO COTTO

PRODUCTION ZONE: *throughout Italy*
MADE FROM: *pork (hindquarters or hams)*
CURING AGENTS: *salt, sugar, pepper, laurel, juniper berries, and spices including coriander, mace, and rosemary*
AGING: *a few days*
FLAVOR: *delicate*

A wide range of cooked ham is produced in Italy. The highest quality ham is made using a traditional method which keeps the meat and muscle firm. First the bone is removed, then the meat is left to marinate in a mixture of salt, salt nitrate, sugar, monosodium glutamate, pepper, laurel, juniper berries, and other spices for the time necessary to absorb the flavors. When produced industrially, this marinating mixture is injected into the ham by machines. The well softened meat is then pressed into molds lined with a special type of paper to give the hams the desired shape. They are then cooked in steam ovens and left to cool in the molds. Curing takes only a few days and the ham is soon ready to be eaten.

In top quality ham, the pink color of the flesh should not be too bright.

Fontina Cheese and Ham Croquettes
(Serves 6)

Ingredients
- 2 cups/500 ml milk
- dash of salt
- dash nutmeg
- 3½ oz/100 g butter
- 3½ oz/100 g all-purpose flour
- 3½ oz/100 g ham
- 3½ oz/100 g Fontina cheese
- 4 eggs
- 7 oz/200 g fine bread crumbs
- 2 cups/500 ml oil, for frying

Boil the milk with the salt and nutmeg. Melt the butter in a heavy-bottomed pan, add the flour, mixing thoroughly. Pour the milk, a little at a time, into the flour and butter mixture, and stir until smooth and dense. Remove from heat, add the ham, Fontina, and two egg yolks. Mix well and leave to cool. Beat the remaining eggs in a bowl then set aside. When the milk and cheese mixture has solidified, shape spoonfuls of the mixture into walnut-sized balls. Dip in the beaten eggs, and then into the bread crumbs. Heat the oil in a large skillet (frying pan) and fry the balls in batches until golden brown. Drain on paper towels and serve hot.

Wine: a dry red (Nebbiolo d'Alba)

Spinach Risotto with Ham and Cheese
(Serves 6)

Ingredients
- 13 oz/400 g spinach, cleaned
- 2 cloves garlic, finely chopped
- 6 tbsp extra-virgin olive oil
- ½ white onion, finely chopped
- 3 tbsp butter
- 13 oz/400 g short-grain rice (preferably Italian Arborio or Carnaroli)
- 6 tbsp white wine
- 6 cups/1½ liters vegetable stock, boiling
- 6 oz/180 g ham, diced
- 6 oz/180 g Taleggio (or Fontina) cheese
- salt and freshly ground black pepper
- 10 leaves fresh basil, torn

Cook the spinach in a little salted water until tender. Drain well and chop finely. Sauté the garlic in the oil until gold. Add the spinach and cook over medium heat for 5 minutes. In a separate pan, sauté the onion with the butter until soft. Remove from heat and add the rice to the onion, stirring so that the grains are coated. Return to high heat and stir in the wine. When the wine has evaporated, gradually add the stock, stirring often, until the rice is tender. Add the spinach, ham, and cheese 5 minutes before the rice is cooked. Season with salt and pepper, and sprinkle with the basil. Serve hot.

Wine: a dry white (Pinot Bianco del Collio)

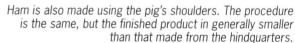

Ham is also made using the pig's shoulders. The procedure is the same, but the finished product in generally smaller than that made from the hindquarters.

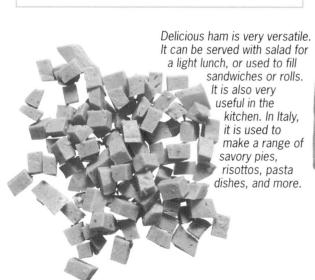

Delicious ham is very versatile. It can be served with salad for a light lunch, or used to fill sandwiches or rolls. It is also very useful in the kitchen. In Italy, it is used to make a range of savory pies, risottos, pasta dishes, and more.

Prosciutto Affumicato

S moked ham is made from cooked ham that has been directly or indirectly exposed to smoke. The cooked hams are first lathered with pork fat, then placed in special chambers for two or three days where they absorb the aroma produced by the slow burning of beech wood. They are then dried for 12 months before consumption. Smoked ham has a very distinctive taste.

PRODUCTION ZONE: throughout Italy, particularly Friuli-Venezia Giulia (Udine)
MADE FROM: pork (hindquarters or hams)
CURING AGENTS: salt, pepper, cinnamon, garlic, nutmeg, rosemary, and sage, smoked for 2–3 days
AGING: 10–12 months
FLAVOR: smokey

Ham has been served in Italy since Roman times, if not before. The first description of how to cure ham was given in Cato's De re rustica, written in the 3rd or 2nd century BC.

The rich, muted flavors of smoked ham are brought out by the nutty tones of whole wheat or rye bread. Serve thick slices on lightly toasted bread with a little butter.

24

Potato Gnocchi with Smoked Ham and Artichokes

(Serves 6)

Ingredients
- 2 lb/1 kg potatoes, boiled and mashed
- 8 oz/250 g all-purpose flour
- 3 egg yolks
- 2 oz/60 g freshly grated Parmesan cheese
- dash of salt
- dash of nutmeg
- 6 artichokes
- 3 cloves garlic, finely chopped
- 2 tbsp finely chopped parsley
- 7 tbsp extra-virgin olive oil
- salt and freshly ground black pepper
- ½ cup/125 ml dry white wine
- 1 lb/500 g tomatoes, peeled and chopped
- 7 oz/200 g smoked ham, diced
- 4 oz/125 g freshly grated Pecorino cheese

Place the potatoes in a bowl and stir in the flour, egg yolks, Parmesan, salt, and nutmeg. Mix well and set aside. Clean the artichokes by trimming the stem, removing all the tough outer leaves, and the fuzzy choke in the center. Slice thinly. Sauté the garlic and parsley in a skillet (frying pan) with the oil until pale gold. Add the artichokes and pour in the wine. When the wine has evaporated, add the tomatoes, check the seasoning, cover and cook over low heat until the artichokes are tender. Add the ham. Meanwhile, prepare the gnocchi by rolling spoonfuls of the potato mixture on a floured work surface into long "sausages" about ³/₄ in/2 cm thick, then cut into pieces about 1 in/2.5 cm long. Cook the gnocchi in batches in a large pan of salted, boiling water. When the gnocchi bob up to the surface remove them with a slotted spoon, drain well, and stir into the sauce. Sprinkle with the Pecorino and serve.

Wine: a dry red (Barbera dei Colli Bolognesi)

Prosciutto Arrosto

Roast ham is made by first removing the bone from a ham. The meat is then cured using a mixture of salt and finely ground aromatic herbs and spices. It is steam cooked, then browned on the outside to darken the color and add extra flavor to the meat.

PRODUCTION ZONE: *throughout Italy*
MADE FROM: *pork (hindquarters or hams)*
CURING AGENTS: *salt, aromatic herbs, and spices*
AGING: *a few days*
FLAVOR: *subtle*

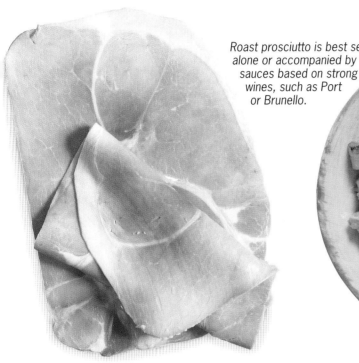

Roast prosciutto is best served alone or accompanied by sauces based on strong wines, such as Port or Brunello.

25

Fricasséed Chicken, Roast Ham, and Vegetables
(Serves 4–6)

Ingredients
- 1 lb/500 g chicken breasts, boned
- 1 leek, finely sliced in wheels
- 6 tbsp extra-virgin olive oil
- 7 oz/200 g zucchini (courgettes) diced
- 7 oz/200 g eggplant (aubergines), diced
- 7 oz/200 g red bell peppers, diced
- salt and freshly ground black pepper
- 6 tbsp beef stock (or water)
- 3 egg yolks
- juice of 1 lemon
- 12 leaves fresh basil, torn
- dash of oregano
- 2 ripe tomatoes, diced
- 4 oz/125 g roast ham, diced

Remove any fat from the chicken breasts and cut into bite-sized chunks. In a skillet (frying pan), sauté the leeks in the oil until brown. Add the other vegetables, and season with salt and pepper. Cook for 5 minutes then add the chicken and sauté over high heat to seal the meat. Pour in the stock (or water) and continue to cook over medium heat. In a bowl, beat the egg yolks with the lemon juice, add the basil, oregano, salt, and pepper. Pour the egg mixture onto the chicken and vegetables, and toss quickly over high heat. Scatter with the tomatoes and ham, toss again, and serve.

Wine: a dry red (Merlot dei Colli Bolognesi)

Speck

Speck comes from the northern Alto Adige region, where both German and Italian are spoken. Although "speck" means lard in German, this pork product is unique. Made from shoulders and hams, it is first boned and then treated with salt, garlic, and varying mixtures of herbs and spices. It is then smoked and aged for 6 months. The smoking procedure, which lasts about 3 weeks, is a delicate operation and requires resinous woods, such as beech, juniper, or ash. Speck has a very distinctive spicy, smoked taste.

PRODUCTION ZONE: Trentino-Alto Adige, Friuli-Venezia Giulia (Sauris)

MADE FROM: pork (ham)

CURING AGENTS: coarse salt, juniper berries, pimento, and black pepper, smoked for 20 days

AGING: at least 5 months

FLAVOR: spicy, smoked

TRENTINO-ALTO ADIGE
FRIULI-VENEZIA GIULIA

The best speck is made in small quantities by farmers. Their special recipes are family secrets handed down through the generations.

Potato Gnocchi with Broccoli and Speck
(Serves 6)

Ingredients
- 1 quantity potato gnocchi (see recipe p. 24)
- 4 cloves garlic, finely chopped
- 1 bell pepper, finely chopped
- ²/₃ cup/180 ml extra-virgin olive oil
- 14 oz/450 g broccoli, boiled
- salt and freshly ground black pepper
- 5 oz/150 g speck, diced
- 2 oz/60 g freshly grated Pecorino cheese

Prepare the potato gnocchi. Sauté the garlic and bell pepper in a large skillet (frying pan) with the oil. Add the broccoli and mix well. Season with salt and pepper, and cook for 10 minutes. Cook the gnocchi in a large pan of salted, boiling water. When they bob up to the surface, scoop them out with a slotted spoon and add to the sauce. Stir in the speck, sprinkle with the Pecorino, and serve.

Wine: a dry red
(Pinot Nero dell'Alto Adige)

26

Speck comes in flattened elongated shapes. The outside is blackened from the smoking and the application of pepper. Inside, the meat varies from dark pink to red in color, with only a little fat around the edges.

Pancetta

P ancetta is made all over Italy and comes in a variety of types and shapes. Made from the belly of the pig, it varies in color from pinky white to dark red in the leaner versions. *Pancetta tesa* is the most common type. It can be made with or without the skin and comes in flat pieces. *Pancetta arrotolata*, *magretta*, and *coppata*, are all rolled varieties. Pancetta is a basic ingredient in many dishes, and is used to add flavor to pasta sauces, risottos, and many meat dishes. English bacon is a form of smoked pancetta, that has only recently become common in Italian cuisine.

PRODUCTION ZONE: throughout Italy, particularly Emilia-Romagna (Ferrara), Lombardy (Pancetta con filetto), and Sicily (Arrotolata dei Monti Nebrodi)

MADE FROM: pork (belly)

CURING AGENTS: salt, pepper, and other spices

Ferrara: salt, pepper, garlic, rosemary

Monti Nebrodi: fennel, oregano, vinegar, chili pepper

AGING: 4–6 months

FLAVOR: savory

Pancetta tesa

Originally from central Italy, this pancetta is first salted then cured for about 20 days. It has a strong salty taste. In Tuscany it is known as *carnesecca* (dry meat), for the toughness that distinguishes it from other types.

Pancetta tesa is made of alternating layers of fat and lean parts.

27

Semolina Gnocchi with Pancetta and Gorgonzola Cheese

(Serves 6)

Ingredients
- 4 cups/2 liters milk
- dash of nutmeg
- dash of salt
- 5 oz/150 g butter
- 7 oz/200 g semolina
- 3 egg yolks
- 4 oz/125 g freshly grated Parmesan cheese
- 5 oz/150 pancetta tesa, diced
- 4 oz/125 g Gorgonzola dolce cheese, chopped

In a saucepan, bring the milk to a boil with the nutmeg, salt, and 2 tablespoons of butter. Sprinkle the semolina into the milk, and cook for 15 minutes, stirring with a wooden spoon. Remove from heat, add the egg yolks and Parmesan. Mix well, then add the pancetta. Use a rolling pin to spread the semolina on a chopping board, then use a cookie cutter or small glass to cut the dough into disks. Place in a buttered ovenproof dish and scatter with the Gorgonzola. Bake in a preheated oven at 400°F/200°C for 10 minutes. Serve hot.

Wine: a dry, aromatic white (Trebbiano d'Abruzzo)

Asparagus, Robiola Cheese, and Pancetta Pancakes
(Serves 6)

Ingredients
For the pancakes:
- 4 oz/125 g all-purpose flour
- 1¹/₄ cups/300 ml milk
- 3 eggs
- butter for the pan

For the filling:
- 2 lb/1 kg asparagus
- 13 oz/400 g Robiola cheese
- 2 oz/60 g Parmesan cheese
- 5 oz/150 g pancetta, diced
- salt and freshly ground black pepper
- 2 tbsp butter

For the béchamel sauce
- 3 cups/750 ml milk
- 3¹/₂ oz/100 g butter
- 3¹/₂ oz/100 g all-purpose flour
- dash of salt
- dash of nutmeg.

For the topping:
- 1 oz/30 g dry bread crumbs
- 2 tbsp butter

Beat the first measures of flour and milk together with a whisk until smooth. Whisk in the eggs one at a time. Grease a small skillet (frying pan) with the butter and place over medium heat. Pour a ladleful of batter into the skillet, tipping it so that it spreads evenly. Cook over medium heat until lightly browned, then flip and cook the other side. Pile the pancakes up in a warm place. Cook the asparagus in salted, boiling water until tender. Drain well, reserving the water. Cut off the tips and set aside. Chop the stems in a food processor. Combine this mixture with the Robiola, Parmesan, and pancetta. Season with salt and pepper. Spread a layer of the mixture on each pancake, then fold it in half and then in half again to form a triangle. Place the pancakes in a large ovenproof dish and dot with butter. Prepare the béchamel sauce, adding 1 cup/250 ml of the reserved asparagus water. Pour the sauce over the pancakes, sprinkle with the bread crumbs and the asparagus tips. Bake in a preheated oven at 400°F/200°C/gas 6 for 10 minutes, or until golden brown.

Wine: a dry white (Albana di Romagna)

Rolled pancetta is used in many stuffed dishes, or wrapped around lean meats such as game before cooking. It is cured quite quickly, so that it doesn't become tough. If cured for too long it becomes hard and salty.

Pancetta arrotolata
Rolled pancetta has a layer of protective fat around the outside which keeps the meat tender. It has a mild taste and contains quite a lot of fat, which makes it ideal for cooking.

Pancetta is often sold in slices or diced ready to be used in pasta sauces or other dishes.

Grilled Scallops with Risotto
(Serves 6)

Ingredients
- 24 scallops
- 20 leaves fresh basil, torn
- grated zest and juice of 1 lemon
- 12 slices fatty pancetta
- 1 small leek, thinly sliced
- 3½ oz/100 g butter
- 13 oz/400 g short-grain rice (Italian Arborio or Carnaroli)
- 6 tbsp white wine
- 1 liter fish stock, hot
- salt and freshly ground black pepper
- 6 tbsp cream

Shuck the scallop shells (if not already open), and carefully remove and separate the scallops and the coral. Rinse thoroughly in cold running water. Scatter the basil and lemon zest over the scallops. Wrap each scallop in a slice of pancetta. Place the leek in a skillet (frying pan) with half the butter, and soften over low heat. In a heavy-bottomed pan, toast the rice with the remaining butter over medium heat, stirring continuously. Pour the wine into the rice and stir until it evaporates. Add the fish stock a ladleful at a time,

stirring continuously. Add the coral to the rice mixture and cook until the rice is tender. Season with salt and pepper. Heat the scallops under a hot broiler, and drizzle with the lemon juice. Stir the cream into the rice and serve hot with the scallops.

Wine: a dry white (Pinot Grigio di Aquileia)

Recently, it has become fashionable to cook pancetta and seafood together. Care must be taken to strike the right balance, and not to overpower the delicate flavor of the seafood.

Guanciale

PRODUCTION ZONE: Lazio, Emilia-Romagna
(Modena, Parma, and Reggio Emilia)
MADE FROM: pork (lean and fatty parts
from the finest cuts)
CURING AGENTS: salt, pepper, spices,
and sugar
AGING: 30 days
FLAVOR: salty, mellow

Guanciale is made from pork meat and fat from the finest cuts stuffed into a casing made from the cheek ("*guancia*" in Italian) and throat of the pig. Cured in the same way as pancetta, using salt, pepper, garlic, and rosemary, it looks like a rather lean type of pancetta stesa. It can be served thinly sliced as an appetizer, or diced and used to flavor other dishes. Guanciale is popular in central Italy, especially in Lazio, where it is a key ingredient in two famous local dishes—Matriciana and Carbonara spaghetti sauces.

Methods of curing guanciale vary from region to region. In Lazio, garlic, sage, and rosemary are preferred, while in Emilia-Romagna only salt and pepper tend to be used.

Veal with Crispy leeks, Pancetta, and Aromatic Herbs
(Serves 6)

INGREDIENTS:
- 2 lb/1 kg rump or topside of veal
- 1 tsp fresh ginger, minced
- 2 tbsp fresh thyme, finely chopped
- 6 bay leaves
- 1 tsp red pepper flakes
- 2 cloves garlic, finely chopped
- 1 sprig fresh rosemary, finely chopped
- 4 leaves fresh sage, finely chopped
- 1¼ cups/300 ml extra-virgin olive oil
- juice and grated zest of 2 lemons
- 8 oz/250 g leeks, sliced in wheels
- salt and freshly ground black pepper
- 8 oz/250 g guanciale, diced
- 1 cup/250 ml white wine
- 8 oz/250 g coarsely ground cornmeal (polenta)
- 3 tbsp butter

Chop the veal into bite-sized pieces and place in a bowl with the herbs and spices. Pour in one-third of the oil and half the lemon juice. Sprinkle with salt and pepper. Set aside to marinate for about 2 hours. Heat the remaining oil in a large, heavy-bottomed pan and sauté the leeks over high heat until cooked but still crisp. Remove and set aside. Sauté the pancetta in the same oil for 3–4 minutes then add the veal and spices. Cook until lightly browned, then pour in the wine. When the wine has evaporated, add the lemon zest and a little water and cook until the meat is tender. Prepare the polenta following the instructions on the package. Melt the butter in the cooked polenta and spoon it into individual serving dishes. Top with the veal, leeks, and pancetta. Serve hot.

Wine: a dry red (Merlot di Lison Pramaggiore)

30

Pancetta Affumicata

Nowadays this meat is also known in Italy by its English name—bacon. Like ordinary pancetta, it is cut from the pig's belly. Cured in flat pieces, it is first covered with spices, aromatic herbs, salt, and pepper, and then smoked. The smoking process is a traditional method, and involves burning aromatic juniper wood and keeping the temperature of the smoke low.

PRODUCTION ZONE: Trentino Alto Adige (Valle dei Mòcheni and Pergine)

MADE FROM: pork (cut from the pig's belly)

CURING AGENTS: salt, pepper, lemon, garlic, white wine, cinnamon, cloves, bay leaves, and juniper berries

AGING: just over 1 month

FLAVOR: aromatic

TRENTINO-ALTO ADIGE

Smoked pancetta, or bacon, has a mellow, pleasantly aromatic flavor. In modern Italian cuisine, it is often used in fish and fruit dishes.

In Italy, bacon is not served in rashers by itself or with eggs, but is used to flavor other dishes. Bacon only really became a popular cooking ingredient in the second half of the 20th century. It is now used instead of lard or ordinary pancetta in many traditional dishes.

31

Squid, Bacon, and Bell Pepper Kebabs

(Serves 6)

Ingredients
- 3 lb/750 g squid, cleaned
- 13 oz/400 g bacon, in thick slices
- 13 oz/400 g red bell peppers
- 20 leaves basil, torn in half
- salt and white pepper
- dash of oregano
- grated zest and juice of 2 lemons
- ½ cup/125 ml extra-virgin olive oil

Cut the squid in rings. Cut the bacon and bell peppers into bite-size pieces. Assemble the kebabs by alternately threading the squid, bacon, and bell peppers onto the skewers. Meanwhile, place the basil in a bowl with the salt, pepper, oregano, and lemon zest. Add the remaining olive oil and lemon juice and mix well. Place the kebabs under a broiler or in a preheated oven at 350°F/180°C/gas 4. Turn frequently and baste with a little of the sauce. Serve drizzled with the remaining sauce on a bed of salad greens.

Wine: a dry white (Cirò Bianco)

Lardo

Lard is fat cut from a pig's back. It is divided into regular-shaped pieces and then "massaged" with a mixture of salt, spices, and herbs. The exact mix varies from region to region; in the Arnad area of the Val d'Aosta in the north, bay leaves are preferred, while in the Tuscan Chianti region, herbs such as sage and rosemary are used. Lard is cured for several months before use. Lard was once the main cooking fat in many parts of Italy. In more recent, health-conscious years, it has been replaced by lighter fats such as butter and oil. However, some special types of lard are now served as appetizers.

PRODUCTION ZONE: *Val d'Aosta (Arnad) and Tuscany (Colonnata)*
MADE FROM: *pork (fat from back and shoulders of pig)*
CURING AGENTS: *salt, pepper, cinnamon, cloves, sage, and rosemary*
Arnad: juniper, nutmeg, bay leaves, and yarrow
Colonnata: coriander and garlic
Aging: Arnad: 3–12 months, Colonnata: 6 months
FLAVOR: *savory*

32

Lardo di Colonnata

This is a special lard made in a small village in the Apuan Alps in Tuscany. It is cured by a layering process and then placed in marble tubs with lids. This produces a marinating liquid which softens and flavors the lard. Served in very thin slices, it quite literally melts in the mouth.

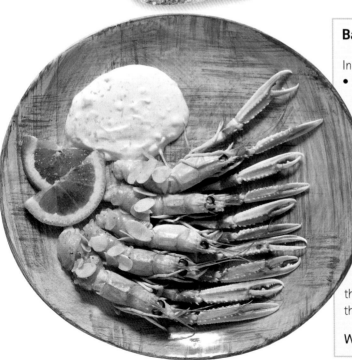

Baked Scampi with Lard and Almonds (Serves 6)

Ingredients
- 24 scampi (small lobsters), shelled
- 12 slices lard
- 2 oz/60 g flaked almonds
- juice and finely grated zest of 2 oranges
- 2 egg yolks
- $^2/_3$ cup/200 ml sunflower oil
- dash of salt
- 1 small stalk celery, finely chopped

Roll each scampi in a slice of lard. Place in an ovenproof dish, scatter with the almonds, and drizzle with the orange juice. Bake in a hot oven for 3 minutes. Prepare a mayonnaise using the egg yolks, salt, and oil, then add the orange zest and celery. Serve the scampi with the mayonnaise passed separately.

Wine: a dry rosé (Rosato di Salice Salentino)

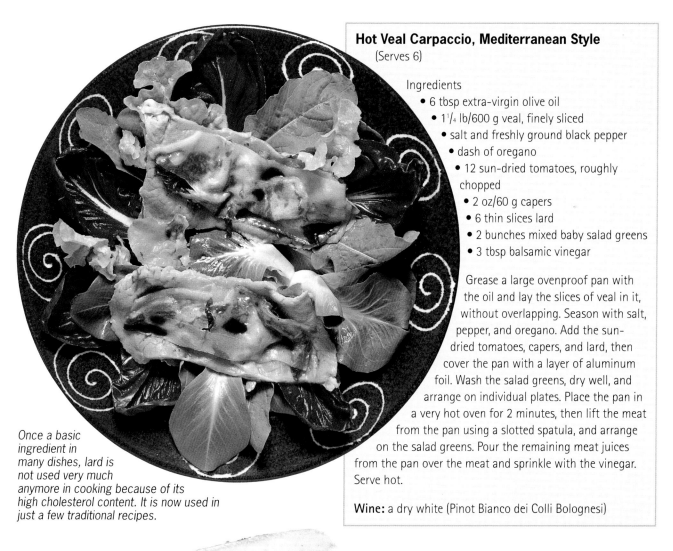

Hot Veal Carpaccio, Mediterranean Style

(Serves 6)

Ingredients
- 6 tbsp extra-virgin olive oil
- 1¼ lb/600 g veal, finely sliced
- salt and freshly ground black pepper
- dash of oregano
- 12 sun-dried tomatoes, roughly chopped
- 2 oz/60 g capers
- 6 thin slices lard
- 2 bunches mixed baby salad greens
- 3 tbsp balsamic vinegar

Grease a large ovenproof pan with the oil and lay the slices of veal in it, without overlapping. Season with salt, pepper, and oregano. Add the sun-dried tomatoes, capers, and lard, then cover the pan with a layer of aluminum foil. Wash the salad greens, dry well, and arrange on individual plates. Place the pan in a very hot oven for 2 minutes, then lift the meat from the pan using a slotted spatula, and arrange on the salad greens. Pour the remaining meat juices from the pan over the meat and sprinkle with the vinegar. Serve hot.

Wine: a dry white (Pinot Bianco dei Colli Bolognesi)

33

Once a basic ingredient in many dishes, lard is not used very much anymore in cooking because of its high cholesterol content. It is now used in just a few traditional recipes.

Lardo d'Arnad

Arnad lard is made from pigs which are fed exclusively on vegetables and chestnuts. It is cured with only the finest local herbs (garlic, rosemary, bay leaves). The lard is then kept in a special container, called a doil, traditionally made by local artisans of chestnut wood. Today steel and plastic containers are also used.

Lard must be cured for at least 3 months before consumption.

Coppa and Capocollo

Coppa is made from the neck muscles of the pig, processed in a similar way to prosciutto crudo (raw ham). Coppa is pressed into a cylindrical shape with pointed ends. It is very compact and quite firm. Inside, the meat is red, interspersed with rosy white pieces of fat. Its characteristic mellow aroma and delicate flavor become fuller and more distinctive as it ages.

PRODUCTION ZONE: Emilia-Romagna (Parma and Piacenza), Umbria, Campania, Puglia (Martinese), and Calabria

MADE FROM: pork (neck muscles)

CURING AGENTS: salt, pepper, and spices (may include cinnamon, cloves, chili pepper, fennel seeds, bay leaves, and nutmeg)

AGING: 3–12 months

FLAVOR: aromatic

In the past the meat was enveloped in a coarse cloth and left to cure.

Capocollo

This deli meat is cured using a mixture of aromatic herbs and spices, together with salt and pepper, which give it a very definite flavor. Vivacious in color, it has a strong aroma and a rich, persistent taste.

Serve thin slices of coppa as an appetizer accompanied by the fizzy white wine from the hills of Piacenza.

Coppa piacentina

Made in Piacenza, in northern Italy, coppa piacentina has obtained D.O.P. status (an EC standard; see introduction). Muscle from the necks of large pigs is used to make coppa. It is made in a similar way to raw ham and some types of salami. Firstly the meat is cured with a mixture of salt, pepper, and spices (such as cinnamon, cloves, and nutmeg) that penetrate the meat during a special "massaging" process. The coppa is then enveloped in pigs' gut and tightly bound. The curing stage, which lasts a few months, is done in special rooms with strictly controlled temperature and humidity levels.

Salame

Many different types of salami are produced in Italy, making it impossible to catalog them all. Shaped like large sausages, wrapped in real or imitation pig's intestine, almost all are made of pure pork. They take anywhere between 2 and 9 months to mature, and can be distinguished from one another by the way the meat is ground (either fine, medium, or coarse), by the spices and other ingredients used to flavor them (garlic, chili pepper, fennel seeds, wine), and by the different curing methods.

PRODUCTION ZONE: throughout Italy, particularly Lomardy (Milanese, Mantovano, and Varzi), Emilia-Romangna (Felino), the Marches (Fabriano), Campania (Napoletana), Basilicata and Calabria (Soppressata)

MADE FROM: pork

CURING AGENTS: may include garlic, chili pepper, fennel seeds, and wine

AGING: 2–9 months

FLAVOR: strong, spicy

Salami vendors in ancient Rome
The bustling streets of ancient Rome were peppered with movable stalls from which vendors sold hot spiced wine, fresh focaccia, hot *puls* (a sort of porridge), fruit, salami, and cooked meats. The busy Romans stopped off at these stalls during the day to grab a bite to eat (much as they do today in sandwich joints, wine bars, and fast food places).

The pork and fat in salame felino is medium ground.

The pork and fat in salame mantovano is coarsely ground.

The pork and fat in salame milanese is finely ground.

When sliced, salama di Varzi is a vivid red with quite large pieces of white fat.

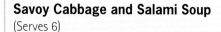

Salame di Varzi

This D.O.P. salami is made in northern Italy, in the area around Varzi, a small town in the Appenines near Pavia. By law, it is made only with pigs from Piacenza (Emilia-Romagna), Alessandria (Piedmont), and Pavia (Lombardy) that have been fed only natural foods. The coarsely ground meat is made up of lean pork from the shoulder, neck, belly, and ham and fat from the jowl mixed with salt, pepper, garlic, and filtered red wine. Wrapped in pig's gut and tied tightly with hemp string, each salami weighs between 1½ lb (750 g) and 4 lb (2 kg). The smaller salamis mature quickly and can be eaten after about 45 days. The larger ones take up to 6 months.

Savoy Cabbage and Salami Soup
(Serves 6)

Ingredients
- 2 cloves of garlic, finely chopped
- 1 white onion, finely chopped
- 6 tbsp extra-virgin olive oil
- 4 lb/2 kg Savoy cabbage, cut in thin strips
- salt and freshly ground black pepper
- 6 cups/1.5 liters water
- 5 oz/150 g salami, diced
- 6 oz/180 g short-grain rice
- 2 tbsp finely chopped parsley
- 4 oz/125 g Parmesan cheese, in thin slivers

In a skillet (frying pan), sauté the garlic and onion in the oil until pale gold. Add the cabbage and season with salt and pepper. Cook over medium heat for 15 minutes, then pour in the water and bring to a boil. Add the salami, followed by the rice and simmer until the rice is tender. Sprinkle with the parsley and Parmesan just before serving.

Wine: a dry white (Pinot Grigio dell'Oltrepò Pavese)

While most deli meats are best served sliced very thinly, salami (especially the smaller varieties) should be cut in rounds just thick enough to stand on their edges.

Rigatoni Pasta with Baby Octopus, Garbanzo Beans, and Salami
(Serves 6)

Ingredients
- 2 cloves garlic, finely chopped
- 1 bell pepper, cleaned and chopped
- 3 sprigs rosemary, finely chopped
- ²/₃ cup/200 ml extra-virgin olive oil
- salt and freshly ground black pepper
- 11 oz/300 g baby octopus, cleaned
- ½ cup/125 ml dry white wine
- 11 oz/300 g garbanzo beans (chickpeas), cooked
- 5 oz/150 g salami, diced
- 2 ripe tomatoes, diced
- 1 lb/500 g rigatoni pasta

Sauté the garlic, bell pepper, and rosemary in the oil in a heavy-bottomed pan over medium heat until soft. Season with salt and pepper, then add the baby octopus. Cook over high heat for a few minutes, then pour in the wine. When the wine has evaporated, add the garbanzo beans, salami, and tomatoes, and simmer for a few minutes more. Cook the pasta in plenty of salted, boiling water until *al dente*. Drain the pasta and cook over high heat with the sauce for 2 to 3 minutes, then serve.

Wine: a dry white (Pinot Grigio d'Isonzo)

This salami is not usually used in cooking because of its very full flavor. In this recipe, the sweet taste of the octopus and garbanzo beans mellows it to perfection.

Salame di Fabriano
This high quality salami with a peppery taste is made in the Ancona province of the Marches, using finely minced lean pork from the ham and shoulder, and small pieces of lard. Lightly cured and not excessively aromatic, it is stuffed in beef or pork gut. It is usually matured for 90 to 120 days before serving.

Size and weight vary depending on the producer, although this salami is generally long and thin. It is generally sliced quite thickly.

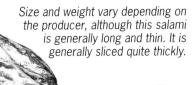

Soppressata calabra

This spicy salami is produced in the south, in Calabria and Basilicata. It is made from the hams of a local breed of black pig. The meat is cut by hand using a sharp knife and then mixed with fat cut from pancetta. The only ingredients used to cure it are salt and chili pepper. Stuffed into pig's intestines, it is left to mature in a cellar for 2 to 3 months before serving.

Salame di Mantova

These small, stocky salamis are made in the province of Mantua, in Lombardy. They have a mellow, lightly aromatic flavor, because of the modest quantities of spices used in the curing process. Unlike other salamis, this one is usually served quite thinly sliced. With the skin removed, the salami is crumbled and used to make risottos and meat sauces.

Salame di Felino

One of the finest Italian salamis, salame di Felino has been produced for at least 200 years in the area around Felino, a town in the hills near Parma. It is made with carefully selected pieces of pork and about 25 to 30 percent fat. The meat is coarsely ground then mixed with salt, whole grains of black and white pepper, and nitrate. Pepper and garlic, ground in a mortar and dissolved in dry white wine, are added just before the stuffing procedure. The salamis are wrapped in special pieces of gut which give them their characteristic truncheon shape. Matured for just 60 to 70 days, they are soft with a delicate flavor.

Salsiccia napoletana

Variations on this dried U-shaped sausage, originally from the Campania region (around Avellino, Benevento, and Nola), are now produced all over southern Italy. It can be spicy or sweet, depending on the amount of chili pepper and fennel seeds it contains. The pork, ground to medium-cut, is stuffed in a very fine natural pig's gut, made without the mucous membrane, and tied using string.

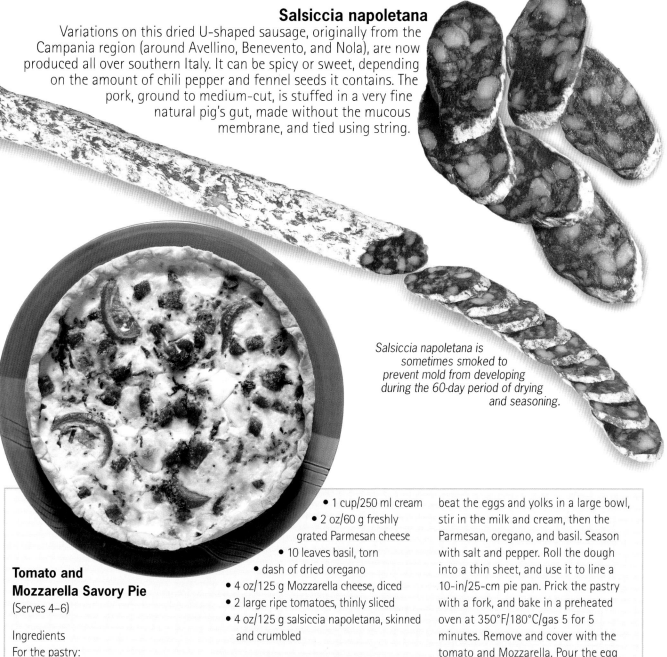

Salsiccia napoletana is sometimes smoked to prevent mold from developing during the 60-day period of drying and seasoning.

Tomato and Mozzarella Savory Pie

(Serves 4–6)

Ingredients
For the pastry:
- 8 oz/250 g all-purpose flour
- dash of salt
- 3¹/₂ oz/100 g butter, softened
- about ¹/₂ cup/125 ml water
For the topping
- 2 eggs + 2 yolks
- 1 cup/250 ml milk
- 1 cup/250 ml cream
- 2 oz/60 g freshly grated Parmesan cheese
- 10 leaves basil, torn
- dash of dried oregano
- 4 oz/125 g Mozzarella cheese, diced
- 2 large ripe tomatoes, thinly sliced
- 4 oz/125 g salsiccia napoletana, skinned and crumbled

Place the flour and salt in a mound on a clean work surface, make a well in the center, and fill with the butter. Work the butter into the flour using your hands. Mix in enough water to make a firm dough. Shape into a ball and chill in the refrigerator for 30 minutes. Meanwhile, beat the eggs and yolks in a large bowl, stir in the milk and cream, then the Parmesan, oregano, and basil. Season with salt and pepper. Roll the dough into a thin sheet, and use it to line a 10-in/25-cm pie pan. Prick the pastry with a fork, and bake in a preheated oven at 350°F/180°C/gas 5 for 5 minutes. Remove and cover with the tomato and Mozzarella. Pour the egg and cream mixture over the top and sprinkle with the salsiccia. Return to the oven for about 15 minutes. Remove when the topping is lightly colored and leave to cool slightly. Serve warm.

Wine: a dry rosé (Solopaca Rosato)

Salame Milanese

SALAME MILANESE

PRODUCTION ZONE: Lombardy (Milan, Codogno, and Brianza)

MADE FROM: pork (50%), beef (25%), and lard (25%)

CURING AGENTS: salt, pepper, garlic, white wine, and spices

AGING: 3–6 months

FLAVOR: subtle, mild

Milan
Codogno

One of the best known salamis, it is made from a mixture of pork and beef, finely ground *"a grana di riso"* (like grains of rice) and then stuffed into natural pig's gut or, when produced on an industrial scale, into synthetic gut. It is cured with a basic, not overly strong mix of salt and spices. Many Milanese salamis are quite large, weighing 7 to 9 lb (3 to 4 kg). They undergo one of the longest maturing periods and are very compact with a nice balance of fat and lean parts.

In Milan, it is usually served thinly sliced with michetta, a local bread roll.

Milanese salami looks and tastes a lot like Salami ungarese (a salame made in Italy to a Hungarian recipe), although the latter is cured differently using more spices.

Milanese salami has much smaller pieces of fat than most other Italian salamis. It is a bright, almost ruby red color.

Salami in Red Wine
(Serves 6)

Ingredients
- 1¼ lb/600 g fresh salame milanese
- ½ cup/125 ml red wine vinegar
- ⅔ cup/200 ml red wine
- 11 oz/300 g garbanzo beans (chickpeas), cooked
- 7 oz/200 g canned tomatoes, finely chopped
- salt and black pepper

Cut the salami into slices of medium thickness. Heat a little water in a large skillet (frying pan) and add the salami. When it begins to sizzle, add the vinegar and then the wine. When the wine has evaporated, add the garbanzo beans. Heat the tomatoes in another pan then add to the skillet. Season with salt and pepper and cook for 15 minutes. Serve hot.

Wine: a light, dry red (Lambrusco Mantovano)

Salame Toscano

T uscan salami is distinguished by its intense aromatic flavor and the relatively large pieces of fat it contains. It is made from carefully selected pieces of pork and pork fat which are coarsely ground then mixed with salt, spices, and whole grains of black pepper. It is stuffed in pig's gut, then left to mature in well-aired rooms for varying lengths of time, depending on size and the taste the producer wishes to confer.

PRODUCTION ZONE: Tuscany
MADE FROM: pork and pork fat
CURING AGENTS: salt, garlic macerated in wine, and ground black pepper
AGING: about 6 months
FLAVOR: savory, intense

TUSCANY

Tuscan salami is usually served with the local unsalted bread, or schiacciata fiorentina (a salty Florentine focaccia). It is also excellent with fruit; figs, and salami are a typical Tuscan appetizer in the summertime. Try it with cantaloupe (melon) and kiwi fruit too.

41

There is also a smaller version, called cacciatorino, which is firmer and more compact. These small, thin salami take less time to mature because of their size.

Sometimes some small patches of mold form on the outside during the drying process. These are signs of genuineness and are easily scrubbed off before serving.

Finocchiona

PRODUCTION ZONE: Tuscany (Florence and Chianti)
MADE FROM: pork (shoulder and cheek)
CURING AGENTS: salt, pepper, garlic, wild fennel seeds, and wine
AGING: at least 5 months
FLAVOR: mild aniseed

TUSCANY
Florence

Finocchiona is a Tuscan salami which takes its name from the wild fennel seeds (fennel is called *finocchio* in Italian) which give the sausage its overriding flavor. Usually made of finely ground pure pork and fat from the pig's jowl, it is mixed with red wine, salt, pepper, and aromatic herbs, then stuffed into a cow's gut. Ground beef is sometimes added to the mixture. The salamis are often quite large – up to 8 in (20 cm) in diameter – which helps them to stay moist and crumbly.

During aging, which lasts anywhere between 7 months and 1 year, mold sometimes forms on the outside. This should be scrubbed off before use.

42

Finocchiona Salad (Serves 6)

Ingredients
- 14 oz/400 g finocchiona, in large thick slices
- 2 bunches arugula, washed and well dried
- 2 stalks celery, washed and thinly sliced
- 1 fennel, washed and cut in small thin strips
- 7 oz/200 g fresh Pecorino cheese, diced
- salt and freshly ground black pepper
- 2 tbsp white wine vinegar
- 6 tbsp extra-virgin olive oil

Cut the slices of finocchiona in halves or quarters. Arrange the arugula on individual plates, and top with celery, fennel, cheese, and finocchiona. Season with salt and pepper. Drizzle with the vinegar and oil and serve.

Wine: a dry red (Chianti dei Colli Senese)

Finocchiona with Polenta (Serves 6)

Ingredients
- 11 oz/300 g coarsely ground cornmeal (polenta)
- 4 cups/1 liter water
- 6 thick slices finocchiona
- 6 Savoy cabbage leaves
- 1¼ lb/600 g fresh or canned tomatoes, peeled and chopped
- 20 fresh basil leaves, torn
- 2 cloves garlic, bruised
- salt and freshly ground black pepper

Pour the cornmeal into a pan with the salted, boiling water, and cook over medium heat for about 50 minutes (or the time indicated on the package), stirring with a wooden spoon. Wrap the finocchiona in the cabbage leaves and tie firmly with kitchen string. Place the tomato in a heavy-bottomed pan with the garlic, basil, salt, and pepper. Add the cabbage packages and simmer for 30 minutes. Serve hot with the sauce and polenta.

Wine: a dry red (Carmignano Rosso)

Finocchiona is usually served as is, in salads, with artichoke, or lightly heated and placed on slices of grilled polenta.

In Impruneta, a town just outside of Florence, a very soft, crumbly finocchiona is made called "sbriciolona." This is the best type of finocchiona, made with leaner meat and aged less. It is always cut by hand and served in thick slices.

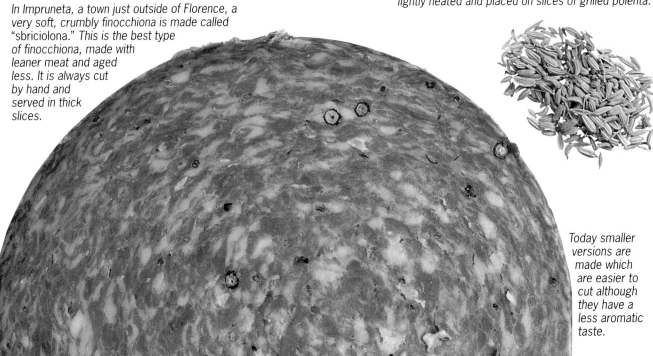

Today smaller versions are made which are easier to cut although they have a less aromatic taste.

Salsiccia Fresca

Salsiccia fresca, or sausages, are made all over the world and are probably the oldest type of deli meat. In Italy, they have evolved through the centuries into many different regional varieties. They are almost always made of pork meat and fat, well ground together, flavored with spices, salt, and pepper, then stuffed into natural gut. The tying procedure, according to the type of sausage, gives them their final form.

PRODUCTION ZONE: throughout Italy

MADE FROM: pork (gut stuffed with meat and fat)

CURING AGENTS: salt and pepper (varying according to the area in which it is produced)

AGING: about 2 months (may also be consumed fresh, raw or cooked)

FLAVOR: varies according to where the sausages are made

Milan
TUSCANY *Siena*
Rome
Naples

Always perforate the skin before cooking so that some of the fat is released during cooking. This will stop the sausage from bursting.

Salsiccia Toscana

Tuscan sausages are made from various cuts of pork, including the shoulder and ham. These are chopped and mixed with natural aromas such as sage and rosemary and then stuffed into gut. Tuscan sausages can be eaten fresh or mature (aged about 1 month). They are usually served grilled or roasted.

Spicy sausages can be eaten raw on slices of bread, or cooked and eaten hot.

Salsiccia fresca al peperoncino

These hot and spicy sausages are flavored with chopped garlic, salt, and chili pepper, which gives them their reddish color. They are usually quite small and compact.

Sausages and Beans (Serves 4)

Ingredients
- 11 oz/300 g dry cannellini or white kidney beans
- salt and freshly ground black pepper
- 12 medium Italian sausages
- 6 tbsp extra-virgin olive oil
- 3 cloves garlic, finely chopped
- sprig fresh rosemary, finely chopped
- 13 oz/400 g fresh or canned tomatoes, peeled and chopped

Soak the beans overnight in cold water. Cook in a large pot of boiling water for 1 hour, or until tender. Season with salt just before they are cooked so that they don't toughen and lose their skins. Prick the sausages with a fork and sauté in a large skillet (frying pan) over high heat for 5 minutes. Remove from heat and set aside in a warm oven. Sauté the garlic and rosemary in the skillet with the sausage fat and oil. When the garlic is soft, add the tomatoes and season with salt and pepper. Add the beans and cook for 10 minutes. Add the sausages and cook for 5 more minutes. Serve hot.

Wine: a dry red (Chianti Classico)

A Florentine dish
Hearty sausages and beans are a traditional dish in Florence. Trattorias in the city still serve this dish today.

Salsiccia al finocchio
Fennel sausages differ from the classic Tuscan variety because they have finely crumbled, dry wild fennel seeds mixed in with the other spices.

Salsiccia di cinghiale
Wild boar sausages are small and compact. They are left to mature in a cool, dry place for a few months. Dark in color, with a strong, yet not over-salty flavor, they are normally conserved in melted fat or olive oil.

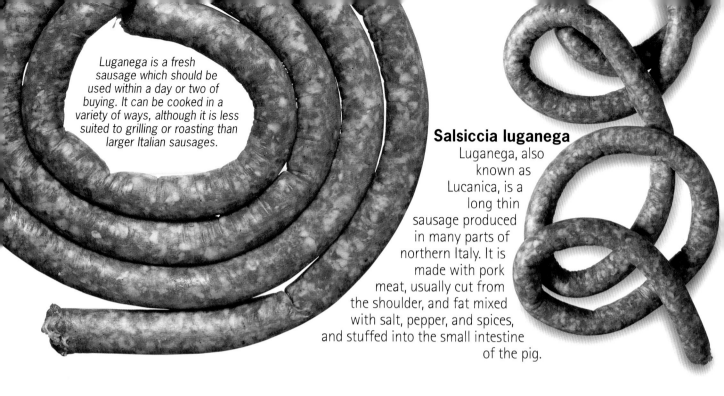

Luganega is a fresh sausage which should be used within a day or two of buying. It can be cooked in a variety of ways, although it is less suited to grilling or roasting than larger Italian sausages.

Salsiccia luganega

Luganega, also known as Lucanica, is a long thin sausage produced in many parts of northern Italy. It is made with pork meat, usually cut from the shoulder, and fat mixed with salt, pepper, and spices, and stuffed into the small intestine of the pig.

Salsiccia Luganega with Polenta (Serves 4)

Ingredients
- 11 oz/300 g coarsely ground cornmeal (polenta)
- 4 cups/1 liter water
- 1 lb/500 g luganega (or very fresh Italian pork sausage)
- 2 tbsp butter
- 1 tbsp extra-virgin olive oil
- 1 small twig rosemary
- 7 oz/200 ml dry white or red wine

Pour the cornmeal into a pan with the salted, boiling water, and cook over medium heat for 50 minutes (or the time indicated on the polenta package), stirring with a wooden spoon. About 20 minutes before the polenta is cooked, pierce holes 1 in (2.5 cm) apart in the casing of the luganega with a toothpick. Melt the butter in a skillet (frying pan). Add the oil and rosemary, and then the sausage. Brown for 3-4 minutes over medium heat, then turn to brown the other side. Increase heat and pour in the wine; as soon as it is hot, lower heat and cover the pan. Cook for about 10 minutes, turning once. Cut the sausage into pieces about 2 in (5 cm) long. Place the polenta in a serving dish and arrange the sausage on top. Discard the rosemary and drizzle the cooking juices over the top. Serve hot.

Wine: a dry red (Raboso del Piave)

Salsiccia di Siena

Siennese sausages are very like other Tuscan sausages except for their strong garlic flavor. Stuffed into natural gut, they are eaten quite soon after being prepared. In Tuscany, they are often used in the stuffing for roast chicken or rabbit.

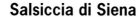

Tagliatelle with Sausage Sauce, Basil, and Pecorino Cheese (Serves 6)

Ingredients
- 1 leek, finely sliced in wheels
- 6 tbsp extra-virgin olive oil
- dash of salt
- 13 oz/400 g fresh or canned tomatoes, peeled and chopped
- 20 fresh basil leaves, torn
- 12 oz/350 g fresh sausage meat
- 7 oz/200 g freshly grated Pecorino cheese
- 1 lb/500 g fresh tagliatelle pasta

In a heavy-bottomed pan, sauté the leek in the oil until soft. Add the tomatoes, salt, and half the basil. Simmer over low heat for 30 minutes, then blend in a food processor. Return the mixture to the pan, and stir in the remaining basil. In a separate pan, cook the sausage meat in a little water until the meat can be crumbled. Cook the pasta in plenty of salted, boiling water until *al dente*. Drain, and add to the tomato sauce. Add the sausage and Pecorino and toss carefully for a few minutes over low heat. Serve hot.

Wine: a dry red (Chianti dei Colli Senesi)

Mortadella

This large sausage, also known as Bologna after the city that invented it, is made of finely ground lean pork (or pork and beef) mixed with fat cut from pigs' jowls. The mixture is shaped into long cylindrical rolls and carefully cooked in steam ovens. The slightly spicy aroma is unmistakable while the flavor is full and well balanced, thanks to the fat which tempers the taste of the meat.

PRODUCTION ZONE: Lombardy, Piedmont, Emilia-Romagna (Bologna), Tuscany, Lazio (Amatrice), and Abruzzo (Campotosto)

MADE FROM: pork (shoulder and jowl) or pork and beef

CURING AGENTS: sugar, powdered milk, gelatin, egg yolks, salt, and pepper, Bologna: pistacchio nuts

Aging: Bologna: not aged Amatrice: 3 months Campotosto: 4 months

FLAVOR: full, lightly spiced

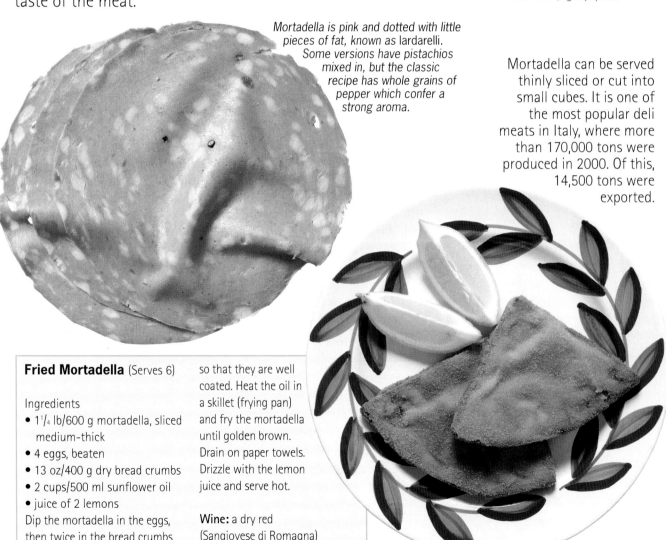

Mortadella is pink and dotted with little pieces of fat, known as lardarelli. Some versions have pistachios mixed in, but the classic recipe has whole grains of pepper which confer a strong aroma.

Mortadella can be served thinly sliced or cut into small cubes. It is one of the most popular deli meats in Italy, where more than 170,000 tons were produced in 2000. Of this, 14,500 tons were exported.

48

Fried Mortadella (Serves 6)

Ingredients
- 1¼ lb/600 g mortadella, sliced medium-thick
- 4 eggs, beaten
- 13 oz/400 g dry bread crumbs
- 2 cups/500 ml sunflower oil
- juice of 2 lemons

Dip the mortadella in the eggs, then twice in the bread crumbs so that they are well coated. Heat the oil in a skillet (frying pan) and fry the mortadella until golden brown. Drain on paper towels. Drizzle with the lemon juice and serve hot.

Wine: a dry red (Sangiovese di Romagna)

Veal and Artichoke Rolls

(Serves 6)

Ingredients
- 12 veal scaloppine (cut from the topside), about 2 oz/60 g each
- 6 slices mortadella
- 12 slices Fontina cheese
- 6 artichokes
- salt and freshly ground black pepper
- 4 oz/125 g all-purpose flour
- $^2/_3$ cup/200 ml extra-virgin olive oil
- 3 cloves garlic, finely chopped
- sprig fresh rosemary, finely chopped
- $^2/_3$ cup/200 ml dry white wine
- 1 lb/500 g canned tomatoes, chopped
- 2 tbsp finely chopped parsley

Beat the scaloppine lightly with a meat pounder, so that they cook quickly and evenly. Place half a slice of mortadella and half a slice of Fontina on each scaloppina. Clean the artichokes by trimming the stem, removing all the tough outer leaves and the fuzzy choke in the center. Use only the tender hearts. Slice thinly and arrange on top of the scaloppine.

Sprinkle with salt and pepper. Roll the scaloppine up and secure with a toothpick. Flour lightly and transfer to a large skillet (frying pan) with the oil, garlic, and rosemary. Sauté for 5 to 10 minutes, then remove most of the oil. Add the wine and cook until it has evaporated. Remove the veal rolls and set aside in a warm oven. Add the tomatoes to the skillet, season with salt and pepper, and cook over medium heat for 15 minutes, or until reduced. Add the veal and cook for 5 minutes more, turning carefully. Sprinkle with the parsley and serve hot.

Wine: a dry red (Barbera dei Colli Bolognesi)

49

Mortadella is used in many cooked dishes, especially those made in Emilia-Romagna. It is a basic ingredient in the filling of tortellini pasta, and also mixed with veal or turkey for stuffing rolled meat, chicken, or roasts.

Mortadella is often made in very large forms that can weigh as much as 110 lb (50 kg). Pure pork mortadella is considered the best quality and is marked with an S (for Suino, or pork) on the trademark. Other types will be marked SB (mixed pork and beef) or SE (mixed pork and horse meat).

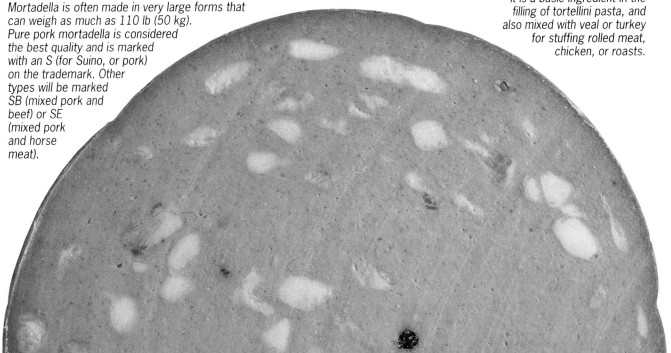

Soppressata

This sausage is made with parts of the pig, such as the tail, tongue, and cartilage, that are not used in other dishes. The coarsely chopped pieces of meat are mixed with pieces of lard and pressed together, then carefully cooked. Found all over Italy, it is known under a variety of different names, including *coppa di testa*. In Tuscany, it is an essential component of a typical *antipasto Toscano* and is also used to fill focacce, bread rolls, and sandwiches. Soppressata can be served in salads (try it in spring with new carrots and celery) and is also used to flavor some baked dishes.

PRODUCTION ZONE: Lombardy (Brescia), Veneto (Valli del Pasubio), Tuscany (Senese), the Marches (Fabriano), Campania (Irpinia, Benevento, and Avellino), Molise (Rionero Sannitico), Puglia (Martina Franca), Basilicata (Lagonero), and Calabria
MADE FROM: leftover pork cuttings (cartilage, tongue, tail, neck, and shoulder)
CURING AGENTS: salt and pepper Fabriano: garlic Martina Franca: white wine
Aging: 2 months–2 years
FLAVOR: aromatic

50

Soppressata and Bean Salad
(Serves 6)

Ingredients
- 3 cloves garlic, 1 sprig rosemary, 2 sage leaves, finely chopped
- 5 tbsp extra-virgin olive oil
- 1 lb/500 g cannellini or white kidney beans, cooked
- 1 head of Belgian endive, diced
- 11 oz/300 g soppressata
- 3 tbsp vinegar
- 4 tbsp finely chopped parsley

In a skillet (frying pan), sauté the garlic, rosemary, and sage in the oil. When the garlic is pale gold, add the beans, and cook for 1 minute. Add the endive, cover the pan, and cook over low heat for 10 minutes. Add the soppressata and cook until the fat begins to melt. Remove from heat and sprinkle with the vinegar and parsley. Serve with thick slices of whole wheat bread.

Wine: a light, dry red (Lambrusco Mantovano)

Soppressata and Potato Gratin (Serves 6)

Ingredients
- 6 tbsp butter
- 1½ lb/750 g potatoes, peeled and thinly sliced
- dash of salt
- 5 oz/150 g soppressata, diced
- 5 oz/150 g Emmental cheese, freshly grated
- 2 cups/500 ml milk
- dash of nutmeg

Melt the butter in a large, heavy-bottomed pan, then add the potatoes and salt. When the potatoes are cooked, add the soppressata and stir well. Arrange the potatoes in layers in an ovenproof dish, alternating with layers of Emmental. Heat the milk in a small saucepan with the nutmeg, then pour it over the potatoes. Bake in a preheated oven at 350°F/180°C/ gas 4 for 15 minutes, or until golden brown on top.

Wine: a dry red (Taburno Rosso)

Soppressata toscana

This sausage is made from the head, tongue, and skin of the pig, cooked in water, then ground, mixed with salt, pepper, spices, garlic, and chopped rosemary. This mixture is stuffed into a round container made of jute, left to cool, and then served sliced. The color varies from intense pink to grey according to the ingredients used.

Soppressata di Fabriano

This sausage has a mellower flavor than the soppressata made in Tuscany and many other areas. Its full aromatic flavor is based on pepper, which is the predominant spice used in the curing process. It is lightly smoked before aging.

Zampone

According to legend, this sausage was invented in 1511 when the city of Modena was laid siege to by Pope Julius II's troops. By stuffing pig's trotters with a mixture of ground lean meat and less usable parts such as ears, skin, and head, the inhabitants made better use of the little food at their disposition. Traditionally eaten at Christmas time, the raw version requires 3 to 4 hours boiling before being served. The pre-cooked variety, wrapped in foil, can be cooked in about 30 to 40 minutes.

PRODUCTION ZONE: Emilia-Romagna (Modena)

MADE FROM: pork (Pig trotter stuffed with lean meat, pig skin, ears, and head)

CURING AGENTS: salt, pepper, nutmeg, red wine, cinnamon, and cloves

AGING: to be consumed within 30–40 days

FLAVOR: lightly spiced

EMILIA-ROMAGNA
Modena

Served at New Year with lentils, zampone is believed to bring good luck throughout the incoming year. It is also excellent with garbanzo beans (chickpeas) or mashed potatoes.

52

Zampone is a mixture of lean and fat cuts of pork flavored with cinnamon, salt, pepper, nutmeg, red wine, and cloves, which is stuffed into pigs' forelegs.

Zampone with Lentils
Serves 6

Ingredients
- 1 medium zampone
- 13 oz/400 g lentils
- salt and freshly ground black pepper
- 6 tbsp extra-virgin olive oil

Rinse the zampone then wrap it in a clean white cloth. Place in a large saucepan of water, and bring quickly to a boil. Reduce the heat to medium-low and simmer for 4 hours. Meanwhile, place the lentils in another large saucepan of cold water and cook over medium heat for about 1 hour. When the zampone is cooked, remove the cloth and carefully cut into fairly thick slices. Season the lentils with salt and pepper, drizzle with the oil, and serve with the zampone.

Wine: a dry red (Pinot Nero dei Colli Piacentini)

Cotechino

This sausage, originally from the Emilian cities of Modena and Reggio Emilia, has become popular all over Italy. The stuffing, made of ground lean and fat cuts of pork and flavored with spices, is similar to the one used for zampone. It is stuffed into pigs' gut and cooked or steamed for 2 to 3 hours before serving. The raw versions also need to be soaked for an hour or two before cooking. Modern, pre-cooked varieties are much quicker to prepare.

PRODUCTION ZONE: Friuli-Venezia Giulia (Musetto), Veneto, Lombardy (Cremona and Milano), Emilia-Romagna (Piacenza)

FRIULI-VENEZIA GIULIA
LOMBARDY VENETO
EMILIA-ROMAGNA

MADE FROM: pork (lean meat, pigskin, and lard)

CURING AGENTS: salt, sugar, pepper, red wine, and various spices

AGING: to be consumed within 30–40 days

FLAVOR: lightly spiced

Mashed potatoes, with a little nutmeg added with the butter and milk, are the classic accompaniment for cotechino.

53

Cotechino Sausage with Puréed Potato and Leeks
(Serves 6)

Ingredients
- 3¹/₂ oz/100 g butter
- 1 medium leek, sliced in thin wheels
- 2 lb/1 kg potatoes, peeled and diced
- 2 cups/500 ml milk
- 1 cotechino sausage, about 2 lb/1 kg

Melt the butter in a heavy-bottomed pan and sauté the leek until soft, but not browned. Add the potatoes and sauté for a few minutes. Pour in the milk and cook over medium heat for 40 minutes. Meanwhile, pierce the cotechino well with a toothpick and boil in plenty of water for the amount of time shown on the package. When the potatoes are cooked, remove from the heat and mash well. Add a little more milk if the mixture is too dense. Remove the sausage from the pan, cut into thick slices, and serve with the purée.

Wine: a dry red (Freisa di Cheri)

Cotechino Sausage Wrapped in Veal
(Serves 6)

Ingredients
- 1 medium cotechino sausage
- 1 slice veal rump, about 1¹/₂ lb/750 g
- 2 tbsp butter
- 1¹/₄ lb/600 g spinach, boiled, squeezed dry, and finely chopped
- dash of salt
- 5 oz/150 ham, cut in thin strips
- 1 cup/250 ml dry white wine

Pierce the cotechino well with a toothpick and boil in plenty of water for the amount of time shown on the package. Drain and set aside to cool. Skin the sausage carefully, taking care not to break it. Flatten the veal with a meat pounder. Melt the butter in a skillet and sauté the spinach and salt for a few minutes. Spread the spinach evenly over the veal and sprinkle with the ham. Place the cotechino in the middle and carefully roll up the meat. Tie firmly with kitchen string. Wrap the roll in aluminum foil and place in an ovenproof dish. Pour the wine over the top and bake in a preheated oven at 400°F/200°C/gas 6 for 1 hour. Slice thickly and arrange on a serving dish. Spoon the cooking juices over the top and serve.

Wine: a dry red
(Colli Piacentini Gutturnio)

Cotechino sausages can weigh anywhere between about 11 oz and 4 lb (300 g and 2 kg). However, most weigh about 1–2 lb (500 g–1 kg). Because the stuffing is quite filling, a medium sausage is usually sufficient for 4 to 6 people.

54

Before cooking the sausage, pierce it well with a toothpick. Do not use a fork for this since too many holes too close together could cause the sausage to break up during cooking. Wrap the sausage in a clean cloth and immerse it in cold water. Bring the pot to a boil over medium-low heat and simmer the sausage very gently. If the skin breaks during cooking, the sausage will fill with water and loose much of its delicate flavor. Steaming the sausage is probably the best way to cook it, although this will take about twice as long.

Cappello del prete
This triangular-shaped Emilian sausage (produced in Parma, Modena, and Reggio Emilia) is named (priest's hat) after the typical hat worn by priests at the end of the 19th century. Also known as *sassolino* or *manicotto*, it is made with the same stuffing as zampone and cooked and served in the same way.

Salama da Sugo

SALAMA DA SUGO

PRODUCTION ZONE: *Emilia-Romagna (Ferrara)*

MADE FROM: *pork (neck, belly, lard, liver, and tongue)*

CURING AGENTS: *salt, pepper, nutmeg, cinnamon, cloves, and red wine*

AGING: *6–12 months*

FLAVOR: *strong, slightly bitter*

Ferrara
EMILIA-ROMAGNA

This special salami, also known as salama ferrarese, is made with a mixture of pork cuts, including the liver and tongue. It is seasoned with salt, pepper, spices, and wine, wrapped in pig's bladder, and cured from 6 to 12 months. Before serving, it is soaked for 5 to 6 hours, then boiled for 4 to 5 hours. It is usually served with mashed potatoes to attenuate its very strong, almost bitter flavor. It can also be served cold with slices of cantaloupe (melon) or figs.

These sausages weigh 1–2lb (500 g–1 kg). Tied with string, a long piece is left at the neck so that the salama can be hung during cooking so that it doesn't touch the bottom or sides of the pot.

A specialty from Ferrara

This sausage is fairly hard to come by. Its production, dating back to Renaissance times, is limited since tradition demands that only one salama be produced from each pig. The only casing suitable for its aging process is the bladder of the same pig. It is a speciality that the natives of Ferrara hold dear.

Boiled Ferrara Salami

(Serves 6)

Ingredients
- 1 salama sausage, about 2 lb/1 kg
- 2 lb/1 kg potatoes
- 5 oz/150 g butter
- 1 cup/250 ml milk
- dash of salt
- dash of nutmeg

Wipe the salama thoroughly with a damp cloth to remove any mold that may have formed during aging. Wrap the sausage in a clean cloth and tie with kitchen string. Tie the sausage to a wooden spoon, and balance the spoon across the rim of a large saucepan so that the sausage is hanging. Fill the pan with water, making sure that the sausage is not touching the bottom or sides of the pan. Bring to a boil, and leave to simmer for 4 to 5 hours, making sure the salama stays well wrapped. About 35 minutes before the salama is cooked, boil the potatoes. Mash them well, mixing in the butter, milk, salt, and nutmeg to make a smooth, fragrant purée. Slice the sausage and serve with the purée potato.

Wine: a dry, full-bodied red (Cabernet Sauvignon dei Colli Bolognesi)

Sanguinaccio and Ciccioli

Sanguinaccio is a type of deli meat based on coagulated pig's blood. It is made by cooking pig's blood with raisins, pepper, salt, grated cheese, pork lard, pine nuts, and rice (or wheat or spelt). In some regions it is strongly flavored with various aromas, including wine, orange zest, rum, and mixed spices. It is then stuffed into pig's gut while still warm and boiled for one hour. It is cut into slices which can then be served grilled or fried. It should be consumed within 15 days. In some regions of southern Italy milk chocolate, candied lemon peel, walnuts, and sugar are added.

PRODUCTION ZONE: Val d'Aosta, Lombardy, Veneto, Friuli-Venezia Giulia, Tuscany (Buristo), Abruzzo, Campania, and Sardinia

MADE FROM: pork (blood, lard, head, and skin)

CURING AGENTS: varies according to region

FLAVOR: varies according to region

Buristo

This is the Tuscan version of sanguinaccio, also known as *mallegato* and *biroldo*, according to which part of Tuscany it is made. The Tuscan version is strongly flavored with spices, including wild fennel seeds. According to tradition, buristo was invented in Siena around 1700 for the soldiers of a German princess who were used to eating *wurst*, a German sausage. Buristo is now made in many parts of Tuscany, although the Siennese claim that theirs is the only authentic product. In Siena, Lucca, and Pistoia raisins, candied fruit, and pine nuts are added to the basic mixture. At Volterra, this meat is traditionally served fried along with fried eggs and bacon.

Ciccioli

These small pieces of dried meat are made from leftover meat, skin, and fat from pigs and geese. They are cooked with a mixture of aromas and spices for quite long periods to remove as much fat as possible. The remaining meat is pressed together in a sort of "cake" or left as thin flakes. They are widely used in regional cooking to flavor savory pies or to add taste to sauces and omelets. They can also be eaten as they are, although they are undoubtedly an acquired taste!

Prosciutto di Cervo

PROSCIUTTO DI CERVO

PRODUCTION ZONE: Lombardy, Piedmont, Valle d'Aosta, Umbria, and Tuscany

MADE FROM: venison (back leg)

CURING AGENTS: salt, pepper, and juniper

AGING: about 2 months (depending on size)

FLAVOR: strong, almost sweet

Prosciutto made from venison is fairly rare and quite expensive. However, production has increased in recent years as more people come to appreciate it. Most venison prosciutto is made from fallow deer in northern Italy and also in the central regions of Tuscany and Umbria. It is made from the hind leg of the animal, which is first boned and cleaned of fat, then cured in salt, pepper, and juniper for about 15 days. It has a rather sweet taste and can be served as a starter with fruit or by itself with bread.

Venison Prosciutto with Kiwi Fruit
(Serves 6)

Ingredients
- 1 bunch arugula, rinsed and dried
- 8 oz/250 g venison prosciutto, thinly sliced
- 6 kiwi fruit, peeled and thinly sliced
- 4 tbsp extra-virgin olive oil
- salt and freshly ground black pepper

Arrange the arugula on a large flat serving dish. Place the slices of venison prosciutto over the top and cover with the slices of kiwi. Mix the oil with salt and pepper to taste and drizzle over the prosciutto and fruit. Serve at once.

Wine: a dry, aromatic white (Malvasia del Collio)

Mocetta
This is a special type of prosciutto from the Val d'Aosta, in the northeast. Now made from chamois, it was once made from the ibex that roam the European Alps. Flavored with salt, pepper, and mountain herbs (like rosemary, thyme, bay leaves, and winter savory) and aged 3 months, it can be eaten by itself or served with thin slices of rye bread and butter.

Prosciutto di Cinghiale

Prosciutto made from wild boar is produced mainly in the coastal Maremma area of Tuscany, and in Umbria where a long tradition of hunting exists. Boar meat, with its strong and very distinctive flavor was once an exceptional treat, but is now readily available thanks to controlled breeding. Aside from prosciutto, other products such as sausages and salamis are made in some parts of Tuscany during hunting season.

PROSCIUTTO DI CINGHIALE

PRODUCTION ZONE: Tuscany (Chianti, Maremma, San Gimignano, and Siena) and Umbria
MADE FROM: wild boar (hams)
CURING AGENTS: salt and pepper
AGING: 4–5 months
FLAVOR: strong, gamey

Salsiccia di cinghiale

These sausages are made from the leanest cuts of boar meat which are stuffed into a casing along with pork fat, salt, pepper, garlic, and Chianti wine. The sausages are aged for 1 month. If they are very hard, they are steeped in Chianti wine before serving.

Prosciutto di cinghiale
The entire ham, including the boar's hoof, is cured intact. Boar meat is lean, compact, and dry and must be sliced by hand.

Wild Boar Sausage Kebabs
(Serves 6)

Ingredients
- 12 wild boar sausages, in thick slices
- 8 oz/250 g Pecorino cheese, cubed
- 6 pickled gherkins, thinly sliced
- 24 small pickled onions
- 4 slices firm-textured bread, diced
- 2 eggs, beaten

Prepare 12 small kebabs by threading pieces of wild boar sausage, cheese, gherkin, pickled onions, and bread onto skewers. Dip briefly in the egg and arrange in a single layer in a large ovenproof dish. Bake in a preheated oven at 350°F/180°C/gas 4 for 15 minutes. Serve hot.

Wine: a dry, full-bodied red (Rosso di Montalcino)

Prosciutto d'Oca and di Tacchino

Cured meats made from goose meat are mainly produced in northern Italy in the regions of Friuli-Venezia Giulia and Lombardy where a variety of products including prosciuttos and salamis can be found. Prosciutto d'oca is made from goose hams stuffed in a casing made from the skin. The prosciutto is salted and flavored with spices such as nutmeg, bay leaf, and pepper. In Lombardy, Marsala wine is added. Aging varies according to regional traditions.

PROSCIUTO D'OCA

PRODUCTION ZONE: Friuli-Venezia Giulia (Udine) and Lombardy (Pavia)

MADE FROM: goose (hams)

CURING AGENTS: salt, pepper, nutmeg, bay leaf, and spices
Pavia: Marsala wine

Aging: Udine: 2–5 months, Pavia: 40 days–2 months

FLAVOR: rich, buttery

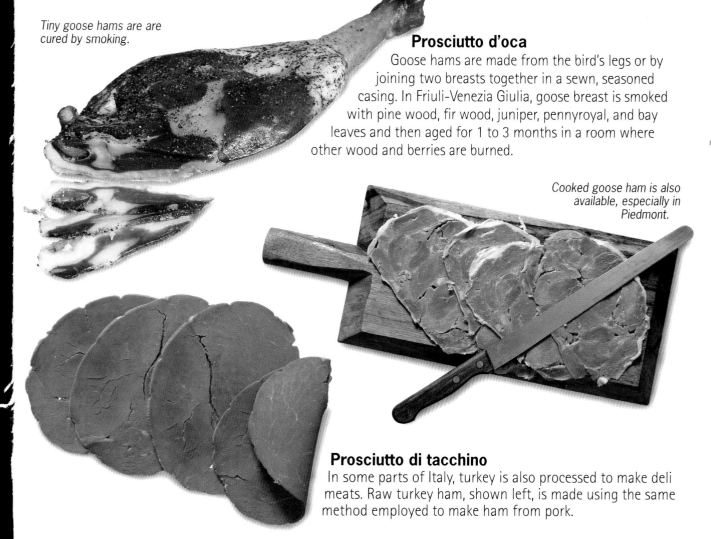

Tiny goose hams are are cured by smoking.

Prosciutto d'oca
Goose hams are made from the bird's legs or by joining two breasts together in a sewn, seasoned casing. In Friuli-Venezia Giulia, goose breast is smoked with pine wood, fir wood, juniper, pennyroyal, and bay leaves and then aged for 1 to 3 months in a room where other wood and berries are burned.

Cooked goose ham is also available, especially in Piedmont.

Prosciutto di tacchino
In some parts of Italy, turkey is also processed to make deli meats. Raw turkey ham, shown left, is made using the same method employed to make ham from pork.

Bresaola and Sfilacci

BRESAOLA

PRODUCTION ZONE: Lombardy (Sondrio) and Piedmont (Novara)

MADE FROM: beef (first quality lean cuts)

Curing agents: salt, pepper, cinnamon, cloves, nutmeg, and rosemary, Novara: thyme, Sondrio: crushed garlic

AGING: 4–12 weeks

FLAVOR: savory, aromatic

resaola, originally a specialty of the Valtellina area in Lombardy, is now produced all over Italy. It is made from lean beef, usually cut from the rump or topside, which is salted, marinated, and then matured, before being served raw in very thin slices. There are also some types of bresaola made from horse meat.

Aging

The meat is salt-cured then marinated in brine for 10 to 15 days. It is then stuffed into natural or artificial gut and left to dry at controlled temperatures that cause the meat to loose most of its remaining moisture. The whole process takes between 4 to 12 weeks. Bresaola that has been aged from 4 to 6 weeks can be served cut straight from the roll. If it has been cured for longer than that, it should be thinly sliced then drizzled with lemon juice, salt, pepper, and extra-virgin olive oil and left to marinate for about an hour before serving.

Bresaola is usually cyclindrical in shape, similar to the muscles from which it is made.

Bresaola di cavallo

This type of horse meat bresaola is made from the ham and rump which has been cleaned of fat and nerves. The meat is then steeped in red wine, salt, pepper, and spices including cinnamon, cloves, and garlic, for 8 to 12 days. It is aged for 1 to 3 months, during which it looses its moisture and a large percentage of its weight. Bresaola di cavallo is produced in Veneto (Padua, Venice, and Treviso), Lombardy (Valtellina), and Piedmont (Novara and Asti).

Bresaola and with Robiola Cheese
(Serves 6)

Ingredients
- 5 oz/150 g Robiola cheese
- salt and freshly ground black pepper
- 2 bunches mixed salad greens, washed and dried
- ½ cup/125 ml extra-virgin olive oil
- 12 large slices bresaola

Season the Robiola with salt and pepper and stir well with a wooden spoon. Arrange the salad greens on individual plates and drizzle with the oil. Spread the cheese on the slices of bresaola, roll up each slice, and arrange on top of the salad greens. Serve with thick slices of toast.

Wine: a dry red (Dolcetto d'Alba)

Sfilacci di cavallo
Sfilacci di cavallo are a specialty made from horse meat in the Veneto region. Thin slices of lean horse meat cut from the ham are cured in salt for 15 days and then smoked for about 1 month. Once the slices have become dry and hard, they are broken up into thin, stringy pieces, hence the name *sfilacci* which translates roughly as "loose threads." A much-sought-after delicacy, sfilacci are usually served sprinkled with oil and lemon juice or on a bed of polenta.

Index

Acknowledgments

The Publishers would like to thank:

Gino Baroni (Florence, Italy); Dino Bartolini (Florence, Italy); Franci e Coppola (Florence, Italy) Mastrociliegia (Fiesole, Italy); La Norcineria (Florence, Italy)

who kindly lent props for the photography.

All photos by Marco Lanza and Walter Mericchi except:
Farabolafoto, Milan: 6A, 6B, 11A
Giuliano Cappelli, Florence: 12A
Overseas, Milan: 13B